The Impact of Absolutism in France:
National Experience under
Richelieu, Mazarin, and Louis XIV

MAJOR ISSUES IN HISTORY

Editor
C. WARREN HOLLISTER,
University of California, Santa Barbara

The Twelfth-Century Renaissance
C. Warren Hollister

The Impact of Absolutism in France:
National Experience under Richelieu, Mazarin, and Louis XIV
William F. Church

The Impact of the Norman Conquest
C. Warren Hollister

The Commune of Paris, 1871
Roger L. Williams

Relativity Theory:
Its Origins and Impact on Modern Thought
L. Pearce Williams

The Impact of
Absolutism in France:

National Experience Under
Richelieu, Mazarin, and Louis XIV

EDITED BY

William F. Church

John Wiley & Sons, Inc.
New York   London   Sydney   Toronto

"*There are favors that time reserves for glorious careers. Useful or ostentatious, their monuments survive them whereas the groans of the generations that were sacrificed to them are soon stilled in the tomb. The memory of Louis XIV is perpetuated by imposing edifices that obliterate many sorrows.*"

Pierre-Edouard Lemontey, *Essai sur l'établissement monarchique de Louis XIV*, Paris, 1818, p. 451.

"*Posterity will involuntarily pause in contemplation before this great reign, astride the paths of history like a two-faced Hermes, offering at once all the attractions and repugnance of absolute power.*"

Ibid., p. 452.

Library of Congress Catalog Card Number: 68-31294
CLOTH: SBN 471 15632 9   PAPER: SBN 471 15633 7
Printed in the United States of America

SERIES PREFACE

The reading program in a history survey course traditionally has consisted of a large two-volume textbook and, perhaps, a book of readings. This simple reading program requires few decisions and little imagination on the instructor's part, and tends to encourage in the student the virtue of careful memorization. Such programs are by no means things of the past, but they certainly do not represent the wave of the future.

The reading program in survey courses at many colleges and universities today is far more complex. At the risk of over-simplification, and allowing for many exceptions and overlaps, it can be divided into four categories: (1) textbook, (2) original source readings, (3) specialized historical essays and interpretive studies, and (4) historical problems.

After obtaining an overview of the course subject matter (textbook), sampling the original sources, and being exposed to selective examples of excellent modern historical writing (historical essays), the student can turn to the crucial task of weighing various possible interpretations of major historical issues. It is at this point that memory gives way to creative critical thought. The "problems approach," in other words, is the intellectual climax of a thoughtfully conceived reading program and is, indeed, the most characteristic of all approaches to historical pedagogy among the newer generation of college and university teachers.

The historical problems books currently available are many and varied. Why add to this information explosion? Because the Wiley Major Issues Series constitutes an endeavor to produce something new that will respond to pedagogical needs thus far unmet. First, it is a series of individual volumes—one per problem. Many good teachers would much prefer to select their own historical issues rather than be tied to an inflexible sequence of issues imposed by a publisher and bound together between two

covers. Secor   the Wiley Major Issues Series is based on the
idea of appr(/hing the significant problems of history through
a deft inter\ \ving of primary sources and secondary analysis,
fused togetf   /by the skill of a scholar-editor. It is felt that the
essence of a   \storical issue cannot be satisfactorily probed either
by placing/   ɔody of undigested source materials into the hands
of inexperi   ced students or by limiting these students to the
controvers   /literature of modern scholars who debate the meaning of so   ces the student never sees. This series approaches
historical   /oblems by exposing students to both the finest historical th   <ing on the issue and some of the evidence on which
this thinl   g is based. This synthetic approach should prove far
more fr(ful than either the raw-source approach or the exclu-
sively s   ɔnd-hand approach, for it combines the advantages—
and avo   ; the serious disadvantages—of both.

　　Final   , the editors of the individual volumes in the Major
Issues /   ties have been chosen from among the ablest scholars in
their f   ds. Rather than faceless referees, they are historians who
know   leir issues from the inside and, in most instances, have
them   ves contributed significantly to the relevant scholarly
liter;   re. It has been the editorial policy of this series to permit
the   tor-scholars of the individual volumes the widest possible
latit   e both in formulating their topics and in organizing their
ma   ials. Their scholarly competence has been unquestioningly
res   cted; they have been encouraged to approach the problems
as   ey see fit. The titles and themes of the series volumes have
be   l suggested in nearly every case by the scholar-editors them-
s(es. The criteria have been (1) that the issue be of relevance
t   undergraduate lecture courses in history, and (2) that it be an
i   le which the scholar-editor knows thoroughly and in which
　has done creative work. And, in general, the second criterion
is been given precedence over the first. In short, the question
What are the significant historical issues today?" has been
nswered not by general editors or sales departments but by the
scholar-teachers who are responsible for these volumes.

University of California,　　　　　　　　　　*C. Warren Hollister*
Santa Barbara

CONTENTS

The Impact of Absolutism in France:
National Experience under
Richelieu, Mazarin, and Louis XIV

INTRODUCTION

Historians of the Age of Absolutism in France have traditionally approached the period by analyzing the work of the French
kings and their ministers. Essentially, the efforts of the royal
government during this period of French national development
took the form of state building for the twin purposes of strengthening royal power over the population and channeling its activities toward a broad and increasingly comprehensive goal—
the good of the state and a higher level of national existence. For
these purposes, the kings and their aides developed newly efficient administrative institutions that provided the indispensable
mechanisms for increasing effective royal power. The royal government extended its controls over the economy of the nation
through well-known mercantilist measures, and it deliberately
influenced the evolution of entire social classes—the clergy, nobility, and the bourgeoisie. It even went so far as to channel the
higher phases of life by fostering intellectual and artistic achievements and imposing religious uniformity upon the entire population. And in their chronic wars with their neighbors, the French
kings succeeded in rounding out the borders of their realm,
thereby providing the territorial basis for national unity and
French hegemony in Europe. These many developments were,
in fact, the most significant in French political experience during
the seventeenth century and have rightly been emphasized by
historians, both because they provided the major dynamic elements of the age and because they laid the foundations of the
modern French national state.

This traditional approach to French history in the seventeenth
century necessarily emphasizes official policy and developments
in the upper strata of French society but tends to neglect the
broader issue, the impact of these measures upon the French

people at large. Specifically, it is infrequently asked whether the
gains that accrued to France during this period justified their
great cost in human suffering and more tangible losses. It is well
known that much seventeenth century state building was not only
dictated from above but was imposed upon the French people,
often in the face of massive opposition from a variety of social
classes. And it is commonplace that conditions of life among the
lower classes—the great majority—worsened as the century progressed. The implication of many studies, however, is that the
results of royal policy were preponderantly beneficial, given the
conditions that prevailed in the period, and that the end, state
building, was of such great consequence that it justified the means
used even though the means were often very questionable. Since
World War II, French scholars have given new attention to the
economic, social, and demographic factors in their national past
and have acquired greater knowledge of these vital phases of
seventeenth-century experience on a mass level. Inevitably we
ask the concurrent question: To what extent was royal policy a
causative factor in determining conditions of life in the period?
Many were undoubtedly beyond the control of any human
agency but, on the other hand, it seems certain that the newly
powerful royal government with its policy of maximum control
over almost all phases of life exercised decisive influence in many
areas, especially those most noticed by contemporaries. Although
the historian can never fully comprehend the past, he should at
least attempt to examine the forces that were operative and,
where possible, assign responsibility to human decision where
this may be demonstrated.

The present volume of readings assumes a knowledge of the
main lines of French governmental policy in the political, economic, social, religious, and international spheres during the seventeenth century. (Royal efforts to promote the intellectual and
artistic elements of classical culture lie outside our consideration.)
Our objective is to present materials—the more significant sources
and commentaries—that will enable the reader to go beyond the
factual narrative and evaluate the impact of absolutism upon the
French people in order to determine whether it was beneficial
and, if so, in what sense. To do this requires the making of historical judgments, a procedure that historians both question and

use freely. In spite of the many problems that the process involves, majority opinion now seems to recognize both the necessity and inevitability of judging the past if one is to attain maximum understanding of it beyond the mere record of events.
Regarding the thorniest problem that historical judgments present—the choice of the proper criteria of judgment—again it is
generally agreed that historians frankly use two standards: that
of the age in question as far it may be recaptured and applied,
and that permitted by historical perspectives derived from a
knowledge of later developments, both being frequently influenced by the historian's own sense of values. Materials to document both approaches are included in this volume. On the one
hand, it should be remembered that contemporaries had the
enormous advantage of knowing their age more fully in many
respects than any later analyst; for this reason, a large number of
primary sources have been included. Expert historical knowledge,
however, is grounded in part upon later, informed perspectives;
thus a choice of the more significant and divergent later commentaries has been added. With the aid of these selections, the
reader may seek to evaluate the impact of absolutism in human
terms as it is revealed by its best historical example, the experience of France in the seventeenth century.

*   *   *

It is axiomatic that the best form of government is that which
is most suited to the conditions of the time and the degree of
political sophistication of the governed. During the seventeenth
century, the various peoples of western Europe enjoyed the benefits of a relatively advanced civilization in many respects but
were, with few exceptions, incapable of self-government. This
was thoroughly recognized on the European continent and, outside of a few small states, there was no questioning of the established order that placed sovereign power in the hands of a series
of ruling families. Not only was the prevailing dynasticism traditional and entrenched; there was no viable alternative. The
result was that governmental authority was held by a number of
rulers who assumed unto themselves all the responsibilities of
political leadership. Because most of the European states clearly

exemplified this type of government in the seventeenth century, one very able historian, Lord Acton, concluded that absolutism was a historical necessity in this period of European development. An outstanding late nineteenth-century liberal, Acton was no admirer of absolutism as such, but he felt that in Europe's evolution from her early, primitive culture to the liberty and democracy of modern times, it was necessary for her to pass through an intermediate period when absolute monarchs channelled her energies and directed her growth.

The case of France is particularly instructive in this respect because of certain important features in her national development that rendered the problem of social control unusually acute and go far to explain the growth of absolutism in her governmental system. For more than an entire generation in the late sixteenth century, France had been torn asunder by religious warfare, which surpassed in ferocity and destructiveness anything that she had previously experienced. During the early seventeenth century, Frenchmen of all classes were haunted by the fear that the realm might revert to its earlier chaos, and there was widespread desire to strengthen the monarchy as the only instrument capable of controlling the turbulent populace. The restoration of peace and strong rule, however, did not mean that the problem of social control was solved. In fact, certain ingrained features of French social organization ensured that unrest would continue unabated on all levels. It was so extensive and endemic in this period that Professor Mousnier has developed the concept of "perpetual crisis" in French society, which he vigorously expounds in our first selection. The social structure of France, he finds, was subdivided into a host of classes, groups, and self-conscious units, that enjoyed various rights and whose interests placed them in continual friction with others in the social hierarchy. Revolts by peasants and workers against fiscal oppression were chronic until very late in the century. In the upper reaches of the social scale, members of the royal family and great nobles developed extensive, quasi-feudal followings by organizing clienteles among persons in various walks of life. Family ties and obligations also continued to be potent and far-reaching. Even certain segments of the royal administration, particularly the parlements, presented effective opposition to the crown, and the Protestant party enjoyed many special privileges that set it apart within the realm. Most important, all these relationships were strengthened by corresponding loyalties whether to class, family, professional group, church, or an individual of high rank and great influence. This in turn meant that loyalty to the state was but one of many competing loyalties that were often strongly antithetical and were sources of continuing friction within the social structure. From this standpoint, a major function of monarchy was to maintain order within a society whose very nature made for disorder and unrest and whose problems were intrinsically insoluble. It should be noted that Professor Mousnier draws his illustrations chiefly from the first half of the century, before absolutism was fully established. If order and stability are viewed as benefits, the continual discord within French society may be regarded as further argument for the historical necessity of absolutism.

In practice, therefore, absolutism entailed not only the growth of effective governmental power through administrative innovations but the establishment of new controls over social, economic, professional, religious and other elements of the life of the people. The purpose of these controls was not only the maintenance of order but the channeling of human energies into endeavors that would benefit the entire nation and cause it to achieve a higher type of existence. In the process, however, both governors and governed recognized that many traditional rights and privileges were violated and the burden upon the populace was vastly increased; yet these seemed the necessary concomitants of such policies. In foreign affairs, the French kings adopted an anti-Hapsburg stance that combined defense of the realm and strengthening of her frontiers with outright aggression in its later phases. To support the resulting wars, which were increasingly frequent, the burden on the lower classes steadily grew to the point of massive exploitation through expenditure of lives and goods. In retrospect, it seems that absolutism, as such, did not necessarily require such policies. For years under Louis XIII, the *dévot* party at court advocated peaceful relations with the Hapsburgs combined with amelioration of domestic problems through a series of much-needed reforms, lightening the burden on the peasantry, and religious proselytizing. The *bons français,* however, supported strengthening the monarchy at home and an anti-Hapsburg policy abroad, postponing reforms and accepting the necessary sacrifices. This group and their policies triumphed under Cardinal Richelieu and left their stamp on French political life during the entire century. To support so costly a policy over several generations in a period when French society retained many socially disruptive elements and its economy was basically agrarian required not only new mechanisms of control but massive exploitation of the lower classes, chiefly the peasantry. Nobles found their traditional prerogatives violated; the peasants were increasingly burdened with the costs of royal enterprises, and significant segments of both classes repeatedly rebelled until Louis XIV's various measures brought this to an end. The great sacrifices that their policies entailed were well known to the French kings and their ministers, but they and their supporters followed the principle that the maintenance of order and the advancement of state interests justified the necessary means regardless of their cost or even their injustice. This means-end rationality was the heart of the widely accepted doctrine of reason of state and went far to justify any measures that rulers and their ministers might deem essential for the general good.

During the long reign of Louis XIV, all these features of seventeenth-century absolutism reached their historical climax. In the years before Louis assumed the reins of government, Mazarin essentially continued Richelieu's policies with indifferent success except in foreign affairs where he won major concessions for France at the Peace of Westphalia. At home, his tenure of power was made memorable by the *Fronde*, the most massive rebellion against absolutism in the century. A major watershed, the *Fronde* demonstrated that intense hatred of absolutism was widespread in French society, but it also showed that resistance of this type was futile, both because of the enormous social and economic disruption that it produced and because it presented no viable alternative to strong monarchy. In fact, the reaction of most contemporaries to the many problems that the *Fronde* precipitated and reflected was that their only solution was more absolutism, and they readily accepted the strong rule of Louis XIV.

It was during Louis XIV's personal government that French

absolutism attained its zenith and exhibited its full potentialities. Throughout the realm, the institutions of government were greatly strengthened, notably by major expansion of the intendants' powers. All social classes felt the impact, and all earlier sources of unrest and rebellion were effectively silenced. The nobles and the Parlement of Paris remained quiescent after their failure in the *Fronde*, and even peasant uprisings dwindled after midreign, in spite of worsening conditions, because of the effectiveness of the royal grip on the provinces. Colbert's mercantilism introduced massive controls over areas of the economy that were formerly exempt from all but local supervision. Religious uniformity was imposed by royal fiat, and a major effort was made to discipline the cultural life of the nation through the work of a series of royally sponsored academies. Most important, Louis maintained an enormous military establishment and embarked upon a series of increasingly costly wars whose purposes ranged from enhancing royal prestige and extending French territory to defense against a hostile European coalition. The great majority of Louis' policies may be interpreted as state-building in the most comprehensive sense, as it was understood in the seventeenth century. His primary purposes combined service to his state with increasing his personal prestige—and it is noteworthy that he generally confounded the two. That he and his apologists readily justified his policies with the doctrine of reason of state was in the nature of things. The benefits that accrued to France were those of triumphant absolutism and were generally admired during the first half of the reign. In the second, however, Louis' personal absolutism increased even further and he clearly overreached himself in many areas, especially foreign affairs. The resulting exploitation of the realm's resources was so enormous that human suffering attained epic proportions, the royal government was utterly bankrupt, and the population of the realm markedly declined. It is not surprising that long before Louis' death his policies were extensively condemned by thinking men, and he died widely hated by the populace. It is for reasons such as these that Louis XIV is regarded as exemplifying both the best and the worst of absolutism. The exact import of his legacy has been debated by historians ever since his death, but there is no denying that it was enormously consequential and determined the course of much French history during the eighteenth century. Not the least of his accomplishments was to fix the form of the French government until the Revolution. On the other hand, the impact of his policies upon the realm was in many ways so disastrous that he lived to see the beginnings of a movement of criticism that ultimately had much to do with the destruction of absolute monarchy.

The selections in this volume represent a wide range of materials with which the reader may assess absolutism's benefits and costs during the reigns of Louis XIII and Louis XIV. Generally the readings fall into three categories. First, a number of sources that illustrate the ideas of men who were part of, or very close to, the royal administration: Richelieu and Louis XIV who shaped official policy, Colbert and Foucault who exercised governmental power in key areas, and Bossuet and Domat whose views of kingship and just rule had a quasi-official standing. The statements of these men provide invaluable insights into the fundamental nature and purposes of absolutism. Second, writings by important contemporary observers. Of these, only Guez de Balzac thoroughly approved of what he saw. The others—Morgues, Joly, Jurieu, Fénelon, and the authors of the report concerning the condition of the provinces in 1687—were among the most important critics of official policy and may be regarded as spokesmen for the large numbers who feared, hated, or distrusted the workings of absolutism. Third, a limited number of important later commentaries that embody valuable perspectives. Of these, Tapié, Voltaire, Pagès, and Goubert present major interpretations of the age while Madelin, Kossmann, Godard, and Cole examine key specific developments. The fact that both the sources and the commentaries contain a wide variety of opinions regarding the precise historical import of absolutism graphically demonstrates that much remains to be determined regarding its exact significance in the period.

Cardinal Richelieu's famous memorandum of 1629 to Louis XIII sets forth the program of action that the king should undertake if he would fulfill the Cardinal's concept of the purposes and obligations of monarchy. Although some of the measures that Richelieu proposes would improve conditions within the state, his emphasis is on increasing royal power both at home and abroad and on using unprecedented measures if these are necessary to achieve his objectives. Such a frank exposition of the qualities and requisites of absolute monarchy by a man who wielded great power is rare in the period. Guez de Balzac, a noted writer who supported Richelieu, effectively argues the case for incipient absolutism by pointing to the benefits that the restoration of peace and order brought France after the chaos of the earlier religious warfare. Mathieu de Morgues, on the other hand, voiced the growing resentment against the Cardinal's "tyranny" by pointing to many of its questionable aspects: Richelieu's extreme ambition and avarice, his riding roughshod over traditional rights and privileges (including those of the members of the royal family), disruption of the social structure, arbitrary imprisonment, oppression of the lower classes, and the inordinate cost of foreign wars. The record of Richelieu's actions gives weight to these charges, but it is noteworthy that Morgues' only recourse was appeal to the king. During the *Fronde*, Claude Joly made similar accusations against Cardinal Mazarin, adding that he was corrupting not only the entire government but the mind of the young Louis XIV. Our modern commentaries on the ministries of the two cardinals present diverse views but seem to imply that absolutism, if not entirely beneficial, was at least justifiable during this period. Professor Tapié expertly reviews Richelieu's legacy, stressing that while it required great sacrifices and remained precarious in its own time, it ultimately made major contributions to the growth of France. Madelin and Kossmann negatively support the same position by showing the great losses and utter futility of rebellion in this age when only strong monarchy was capable of fulfilling the functions of government.

It should be noted that all these authors, except Madelin and Kossmann, are concerned with the issue of reason of state, either explicitly or implicitly. Cardinal Richelieu unabashedly asserts that the justice of kings differs from that in force among private individuals. Religious morality should control the actions of subjects, but the concerns of kings as kings are immediate and practical and they should punish offenders from the standpoint of public necessity rather than Christian charity. The crucial implication was that traditional morality guided the lives of the people but kings might dispense with it when this was required for the good of the state. In essense, the position recognized two levels of morality, one for the people and another for their rulers. Guez de Balzac carried this further by insisting that the king might bypass ordinary judicial procedures and imprison or otherwise punish anyone who was merely suspected of disloyalty. He asserts that the individual may be sacrificed for the good of the state if the sovereign so orders, and he explicitly maintains that the end—the general good—justifies highly questionable means. Balzac was one of the earliest French writers who unequivocally supported the doctrine of reason of state. Morgues, on the other hand, criticized Richelieu's policies as not only tyrannical but morally wrong regardless of any political justification. This position was developed at considerable length during the *Fronde* by Joly who argued that kings and all others are equally bound by principles of Christian morality, and he specifically denied the existence of two levels of justice, one for kings and the other for subjects. His position was supported by the time-honored principle of the universality of justice, as Joly makes abundantly clear. The fusion of law, justice, and morality in the thought of the period enabled the Cardinals' critics to condemn their innovations and socially disruptive policies as both illegal and immoral. The fact that Richelieu and Balzac justified royal policy by arguing its necessity rather than its justice indicates their awareness that it ran counter to tradition in many ways and could be vindicated only by a new ethic of state action. Finally, it may be noted that certain echoes of reason of state are to be found in Professor Tapié's analysis of Richelieu's legacy. When Tapié argues that the Cardinal's policies required great sacrifices for uncertain gains but ultimately contributed much to the building of France, he implies that the latter goes far to justify Richelieu's high-handed procedures.

The writings from the period of Louis XIV's personal rule contain a wider variety of materials but are concerned with many of the same issues. Louis' *Memoirs* set forth his ideal of absolutism in which the king is paternalistic, authoritarian, and responsible only to God. Strong rule is justified by the need of controlling the populace, which must be disciplined. In this piece, Louis recognizes the great responsibilities of his office and also gives special attention to his personal magnificence and glory which, in fact, determined many of his policy decisions. Bishop Bossuet vividly defines divine-right absolutism as authoritarian rule over docile and obedient subjects according to the canons of justice, the latter being a combination of discipline and equity. Jean Domat, one of the ablest jurists of the age, gives a picture of the ideal absolute state in which all is ordered and disciplined from above, again according to justice. The workings of absolutism in key areas are discussed by Colbert and Foucault. Colbert outlines his mercantilist program in terms that unmistakably stamp it as the economics of absolutism, while Foucault gives a vivid and memorable picture of the persecution of the Huguenots and the coercion that was required to restore religious uniformity. All these sources provide extensive insights into the theoretical nature and practical workings of absolutism. Its impact upon the state at large, however, was another matter, and here the report concerning the condition of certain provinces in 1687 contains information that may have surprised even Louis XIV. Its authors give a remarkably frank appraisal of the sacrifices that royal policy imposed on the populace and do not hesitate to single out excessive taxation as primarily responsible, even going so far as to warn the king that he was undermining the strength of his realm. On the basis of this excellent evidence, it would seem that in 1687 Louis was already exacting great sacrifices from the nation.

Criticism by contemporary observers is represented by a chapter from the famous *Soupirs de la France esclave* and two of Fénelon's key writings. The *Soupirs* were written by a Calvinist in exile, possibly Pierre Jurieu. Although its charges are in some measure exaggerated, it contains large elements of truth that the reader will do well to identify, since they strike home in many instances and, in any case, are indicative of the growing hostility to Louis XIV's brand of absolutism. Even more severe are the criticisms levelled by Archbishop Fénelon. His first piece vividly describes conditions in the French army in the north during the War of the Spanish Succession, indicating the exhaustion of the realm as well as some of the sacrifices that Louis' foreign policy required of the populace. His other, more important writing is a massive critique of Louis' rule, written for the heir to the throne by a keen observer and moralist who desperately sought to reverse the thrust of royal policy, which he regarded as disastrous in every essential. And like the earlier critics of absolutism in action, Fénelon specifically denounces the doctrine of reason of state whose intrinsic immorality he finds intolerable and ultimately responsible for most of France's woes. Although Fénelon was one of the most thoroughgoing and vocal of Louis XIV's critics during the latter part of the reign, it may easily be shown that he served as spokesman for a significant and growing body of opinion.

As always, our later historians' commentaries on the reign exhibit a wide variety of views concerning the significance of Louis XIV's absolutism. Voltaire's chapter from his famous *Age of Louis XIV* describes Louis' internal reforms and may be regarded as the classic statement of his accomplishments as a great builder of France. Voltaire offers extensive evidence in support of this view, and he had the advantage of living in an age when Louis' legacy was everywhere to be seen. Georges Pagès, on the contrary, presents a thorough critique of the insufficiencies of Louis XIV's absolutism, stressing its cost to France, Louis' inability to give his work national foundations, and his responsibility for the ultimate destruction of absolute monarchy. The two views contrast sharply in almost every essential and the reader should attempt to weigh their respective merits, since they embody the two most important general interpretations of the historical significance of Louis XIV's reign in the growth of the French nation. Charles Godard analyzes the vital role of the intendants as instruments of absolutism in action, and Charles Cole shows how limited was Colbert's success in his efforts to strengthen the economy of the state. Both authors' views have direct bearing upon the question of absolutism's impact and benefits. Finally, Professor Goubert examines the condition of France in 1715 from the standpoint of the demographer and social scientist. Although he recognizes the depths to which France had sunk at the end of the reign, he emphasizes compensating factors and shows that the decline was not universal. On the other hand, by stressing the latent strength in French society and her economy, he implies that France merely needed a period of peace in which to recuperate from the ravages of Louis XIV's absolutism. The statistics of the very active school of French economic and social historians led by Professor Goubert may seem overly objective in the sense that they do little to indicate the personal experiences of the thousands who felt the impact of Louis XIV's policies, but even his type of evidence indicates that France may have paid an excessive price for her greatness under Louis XIV's rule.

PART ONE

The Problem of Social Unrest in
Seventeenth-Century France

1

Roland Mousnier
The Permanent Crisis in French Society

Roland Mousnier is one of the ablest and most active authorities on the history of France in the seventeenth century. A professor of modern history at the Sorbonne, he has published a large number of books and articles on institutional, social, economic, and intellectual developments during the period. In recent years, he has undertaken extensive research into the popular uprisings that occurred in France during most of the sixteenth, seventeenth, and eighteenth centuries, and he heads a large cooperative project to investigate this important social phenomenon at the Centre de Recherches sur la Civilisation de l'Europe Moderne at the Sorbonne. Professor Mousnier is therefore excellently equipped to analyze the structure of French society and the tensions and frictions within it. These he finds so fundamental and endemic that he views France as plagued by a perpetual social crisis through the final centuries of the old monarchy. The entire, general work here excerpted is structured about this concept. In applying this interpretation to the seventeenth century, he chooses his illustrations chiefly from the ministries of Cardinals Richelieu and Mazarin, but many of the factors that he discusses were at least latent during Louis XVI's personal rule. From this standpoint, it may be argued that strong monarchy was a necessity during the entire period if only to keep the unruly population in order.

Everywhere rebellion was latent and frequently burst forth. Civil war, both potential and actual, was permanent.

In France, the struggle for independence from the Hapsburgs' efforts for hegemony constantly kept the king in financial straits. The available margin left by production was very limited; taxes were always insufficient, the deficit chronic, and every increase

SOURCE. Roland Mousnier, *Les XVIe et XVIIe siècles*, Paris: Presses Universitaires de France, 1954, pp. 160–166. Translated for this book by William F. Church. Reprinted by permission of Presses Universitaires de France and the author. Copyright 1953 by Presses Universitaires de France.

in taxation sharply felt. Fiscal policy quickly became the reason, motive, or pretext for rebellion.

Peasant uprisings were constant. There was not a year when they did not appear in at least one province. Sometimes they became more serious and expanded. From 1636 to 1639, when the open war that Richelieu waged [against the Hapsburgs] increased the burden of taxation, veritable peasant wars broke out in whole regions. It was said that in some places the peasants ate grass, went naked, and committed suicide. The Croquants in Limousin, Poitou, and Angoumois, in groups of 7 to 8000 men, fell upon tax collectors and hacked to pieces an agent for the *aides*.[1] In 1637, they rebelled in Gascony and Périgord and it was necessary to send an army against them. Two hundred perished on their barricades. In 1638, the establishment of the salt tax in lower Normandy caused the insurrection of the Nus-Pieds. These peasants killed the collectors of the heaviest direct tax, the *taille*, and sought to prevent the collection of all taxes that had been established since the death of Henry IV.

The workers in the cities also revolted when bread was dear, unemployment extensive, and taxes heavy. Riots were frequent after 1598. They became insurrections in Lyon in 1623, 1629, 1633, and 1642; the same was true in Paris in 1633 and in 1634 at Rouen where a cobbler led the rope and papermakers in an assault on the *Bureau des Fermes* and in 1639 when the drapers and dyers, led by a clockmaker, attacked the agent of the office that regulated the dying of cloth, a right farmed out to local contractors. The mob pierced the agent with spikes and dragged carts over his body. Then they sacked the Bureau of the Treasurers of France and stormed the home of Nicolas Le Tellier, receiver general of the salt tax.

Instances of insurrection were innumerable between 1630 and 1659, during the Thirty Years' War to 1648 and then the war against Spain.

These revolts were not a war of the poor against the rich. Tax collectors were assaulted, but rarely chateaux and town mansions and, in such cases, it was usually a question of properties of the

---

[1] For the meanings of untranslated French terms, see the list at the end of this volume.

newly rich, officials, and financiers. The revolts were directed against the royal treasury. They became genuinely dangerous to the government only when other social classes participated. As long as the magistrates in the parlements, the *présidiaux, bailliages,* and *sénéchaussées* did their duty, and as long as the bourgeois militia fired on the common people and the nobles did not join the peasants, the king easily reestablished order. But under certain circumstances persons of all classes were found in rebellion and the state was in danger.

Monsieur, the king's brother, and the princes of the blood, heirs to the throne after him, claimed to participate in the government, to play a major role in the king's council, to be masters in the provinces like governors with hereditary titles, to regard the king as only the first of their number or a sort of president, and frequently revolted against monarchical absolutism. Now, more and more, their insurrections involved the commonality, even including the peasants. In this society, sentiments of vassalage and the custom of personal ties between man and man continued vital, as relations between suzerain and vassal. Princes of the blood and great nobles had vast clienteles of nobles and commoners who had given themselves to their lords; sworn complete fidelity and absolute devotion to them; fought for them in duels, brawls, and pitched battles; spoken, written, and intrigued for them; followed them in disaster; and caused themselves to be imprisoned and killed for them. In return, the master sometimes nourished and clothed them, confided in them, always advanced them in society, obtained positions for them, arranged their marriages, protected them, freed them from prison, and stipulated favorable terms for them in the treaties with the king that terminated the revolts. These reciprocal duties took precedence over all others, even the obedience owed the king and service of the state. The king himself was able to make himself obeyed only through the medium of such devoted and nurtured followers who in turn were his own men.

The princes of the blood and the great nobles won followers by having offices at their disposal. Monsieur, the queen, the princes and princesses in their households and *apanages,* princes of the blood and great nobles as important officials in the royal household whose great offices rarely left certain families—all carried things

to the point where some feared that the nobles would surround
the king with kidnappers and assassins. Princes and great nobles
were governors of the same provinces for generations. They
appointed governors of cities, captains of strongholds and citadels,
officers of regiments and companies, and numerous judicial and
financial officials. Ties of interest and devotion arose between the
great nobles in certain provinces, such as the Longueville in Normandy and the Montmorency in Languedoc, and thousands of
families, noble and commoner, of the sword and the robe. From
father to son, thousands of families were "pledged," "bound,"
and "dedicated" to the great and served them better than they
served the king.

Often these faithful followers were themselves holders of portions of the royal domain that they had acquired with the right
to appoint or nominate holders of royal offices and noble judge-
ships with their officials. They acquired influence over petty
nobles, citizens of the smaller towns and peasants, all of whom
aspired to the various types of offices that were everywhere in
the countryside.

Finally, all these lords had enormous influence over their peasantry. Ties similar to those of vassalage united them; the peasant
often felt sentiments of fidelity and devotion toward the lord.
Only if the latter were very bad would the peasants regard him
with hatred and a menacing attitude. On his side, the lord might
render life agreeable or intolerable to the peasants by means of
his judicial and police officers who regulated all activity. Besides,
lord and peasant had common interests against the king and his
fiscal policy. Royal taxation caused rents to stand at a lower level
than they would have otherwise; in bad years it compromised the
collection of interests, dues, and rents. How many times did
the nobles call the peasants to rebel against the tax collectors? The
lords protected their peasants, caused them to be exempted from
tolls and labor, armed them during the civil wars, and led them
in protecting the cattle and harvests. It was rarely in the peasants'
interest to be against the lord when the royal troops pillaged like
all others and the unprotected peasant was certain to be victim-
ized. Most often, the peasants followed the lords.

Besides, every revolt spread the more easily because there was
no strict separation of social classes. In the same family there

were frequently some members of the robe and others of the sword, some married into merchant families and others into jurists', some already ennobled, and others still commoners. From the merchants to the high nobility there extended binding ties that were very powerful during this time of strong family organization and when, moreover, the habit of forming clienteles easily transformed a tie of blood or marriage, no matter how remote, into an obligation of both service and protection.

The king was not even sure of his officials. The members of the sovereign courts, especially the parlements, felt themselves threatened by the creation of other offices that lessened the value and importance of theirs and by increases in levies on their offices that forced them into burdensome loans. As owners of rented lands they were hurt by increases in direct taxes, and they were personally subject to indirect taxes. They therefore refused to enregister fiscal edicts and paralyzed the monarchy's action during full-scale war. The Parlement of Paris claimed to be heir to the ancient *curia regis*. It sought on its own initiative to consider political matters and of its own authority to assemble the princes of the blood, dukes and peers, and officers of the crown to discuss matters of state, as it did fruitlessly in 1615 and 1648. This would have reconstituted the old *curia regis*, the assembly of vassals. To assert the principle that they could come together on their own and make valid decisions was to create a monarchy tempered by aristocracy, whereas the king sought to be absolute and the ruler of all.

In both politics and legislation, the Parlement, a court of justice, sought to become a power independent of the king, to act on its own initiative, deliberate separately, and impose its decisions. It wished to assemble the other royal officials to discuss affairs of state (Decree of Union, May 13, 1648). The Parlement attempted to reexamine, without the king, the edicts that had been verified in the sovereign's presence in a *lit de justice* that reconstituted the old *curia regis*. With its decrees, the Parlement modified or revoked edicts or their individual articles that had been confirmed in a *lit de justice*. It acknowledged the *lit de justice* only as a form of visit by the king who sought their advice on questions of general policy. It declared that the king's presence violated freedom of the franchise and sought to deliberate and vote on edicts and ordinances alone, without the king.

To call together spontaneously the representatives of the realm, discuss all affairs, and vote laws without the sovereign was to erect an assembly separate from the king with legislative power and control of the executive; it was an imperfect outline of separation of powers. The Parlement moved toward tempered monarchy and even opened the way for a republic. Its action was contrary to the existence of monarchy in which king and kingdom formed a whole. The presence of the king did not violate the freedom of opinion of the members of the *curia regis* because the *curia*, the epitome of the realm, could not exist without the king. The king ordered the chancellor to gather the opinions of its members, but he himself then declared the essential will of the *curia* and made it his own. This will might differ from those that had been openly expressed, and the king might decide against the majority opinion. The Parlement's attitude was therefore revolutionary. It was a fundamental disruption, an intellectual separation of two elements in reality united, inseparable and indispensable, the king and the realm, sovereign and nation, a single being. It was a denial of monarchy.

But this political revolution was a medium of social conservatism. The Parlement's objective was merely the preservation of positions that had been acquired by its members, their relatives, in-laws, and equals, as well as those held by provincial and local powers and by owners of offices and fiefs against another revolution, the centralizing and, to a certain extent, egalitarian revolution by absolute monarchy. The Parlement fought against the tendency to substitute the commissioner for the official, the royal council for the sovereign courts, and the intendant for various judicial and financial bodies. It denied that the council alone, in the king's absence, had the right to act as highest court of the realm and to annul any decree of the parlements contrary to royal authority or the public good. It sought the suppression of the intendants who were not content merely to examine matters in order to refer them to the regular judges but gave judgment by virtue of authorization by the council, who dispossessed *présidiaux, prévôts*, and councils in the *bailliages* and *sénéchaussées* of their functions and took over those of financial officials, Treasurers of France, *élus*, and others. The Parlement demanded that these officials be reinstated in their duties of office and that they not be deprived of their functions by mere *lettre de cachet* but only by cases in court according to royal ordinances. It was a question of knowing who was to administer the realm: the royal functionaries who were appointed and dismissed at will and acted in the name of the public good, reason of state, and in the king's interest, which they identified with the general interests of the realm; or bodies of officials who owned their offices, were therefore intractable and practically irremovable, more concerned with the interests that they represented than the public good; hereditary, entrenched, possessing fiefs, enjoying all the powers of lords, allied or related to nobles of the sword, holding power in the provinces, of very restricted outlook, and more representative of the provinces and special interests against the king than the king was against the interests of individuals and the provinces.

The Parlement possessed an effective means of action: to protest against taxes and persuade the French that they were taxed too heavily and unjustly merely for the glory of the king and the luxury of the court, even though the Hapsburgs' pretensions to universal dominion imperilled the very existence of the realm and the wretched court lacked money for its maintenance. The common people therefore developed a sentimental attachment for the Parlement and a sort of veneration. The same was true of the middle-class city dwellers who were burdened by taxes, forced loans, commercial monopolies and the importation of manufactured products. Moreover, the members of the Parlements were colonels and captains of the urban militia. As landed proprietors, they held authority over the peasants on their lands. In Paris during the *Fronde*, the peasants from Saint-Ouen and other villages were called up by their overlords, bourgeois Parisians, and fought in the ranks of the city dwellers in the capital.

The political organization of the Protestant party gave its leaders and municipalities unusual power. The Edict of Nantes granted the Protestants fortified strongholds and garrisons. But contrary to the edict, the Protestants had added provincial assemblies and a general assembly. They divided France into

eight military districts and had a supreme general and an ambassador at court. They formed a state within the state and rendered France a federation composed of a Catholic and a Protestant state, two different peoples united only by a common
sovereign, a political dualism. This federation, which was also
the essence of the aristocratic "feudal" movements, was incompatible with the needs of the state. The Protestant lords took advantage of it to join every movement of the great nobles and
revolted whenever the king was engaged against a foreign power
and needed internal peace.

In certain instances, a union of nobles, officials, city dwellers,
and peasants was formed against the king and his followers. At
a mere signal from a prince of the blood, whole provinces joined
one after another. Then the nobles called the people to arms. The
parlements gave the example by throwing open the granaries
where the intendants had gathered wheat for the army (Dauphiné, 1630) or the royal coffers so that they themselves might
take their wages that had been withheld for military purposes
(Toulouse, 1630). They encouraged disorders, were remiss in
informing against the rebels, opposed measures taken against
them, and allowed the populace free rein as long as they attacked
only royal officials and their properties and spared those of the
other subjects of the king.

Such instances occurred chiefly during the minorities of Louis
XIII and Louis XIV. Political ties seemed to dissolve as though
men had been bound only to the person of the deceased king
and owed nothing to his underage successor, as though with the
death of the king there was no longer state nor law. Many citizens ceased to obey; nobles and commoners fortified their homes,
formed bands, assaulted, and robbed. These occasions were pro-
pitious for the claims of the princes of the blood. They were also
periods of bad harvests and famines and/or wars when the burden
of taxation was crushing and foreigners continually intrigued
with the princes of the blood. At such times, it seemed that the
national spirit degenerated. In accordance with the old idea that
the vassal might choose his lord, Gaston d'Orléans, Cinq-Mars,
and Condé entered into agreements with the King of Spain. The
Parlement, other officials, middle-class citizens, common people,
everyone forgot the enemy abroad. Provinces and cities rebelled

at will. The king seemed reduced to the position of a lord whose remaining strength depended on certain devoted followers and loyal commanders who retained some troops for him, as well as the disagreements among the rebellious princes. Many a time the fate of the realm depended on the fortune of a single battle such as that at Lens which was won against the Spanish in 1648. In the midst of the bourgeoning *Fronde*, no one could tell what would have happened if this battle had been lost. The most likely outcome would have been the dismemberment of the realm and the disappearance of France.

PART TWO

The Ministries of Richelieu and Mazarin

SOURCES

1

Richelieu
A Program for the King

Among Cardinal Richelieu's many analyses of the policies that he advocated for Louis XIII, the one here excerpted is one of the most valuable. It was dictated by Richelieu in 1629 shortly after the fall of La Rochelle and summarizes both the position of French political affairs and the policies that he urged Louis to adopt in order to increase his power and fulfill his obligations to the state. In this way, it gives a remarkable picture of the mentality of one of the principal architects of French absolutism. The brief portions that are presented here not only include Richelieu's insistence upon increasing royal power and enforcing obedience within the realm. They also show that Richelieu, although a high-ranking churchman, recognized that the policies that he advocated might be justified only by placing the interests of the state above all other considerations. Such was his consistent position throughout his long tenure of power from 1624 to 1642. It won him the applause of the proponents of absolutism, but it also provided a basis for extensive criticism of his actions. The future lay with him, however, in the sense that both his policies and his justification of them foreshadowed similar measures on the part of Louis XIV.

SOURCE. This document is printed in *Mémoires du Cardinal de Richelieu*, Paris, 1929, Vol. IX, pp. 14–59, and in *Lettres, instructions diplomatiques et papiers d'état du Cardinal de Richelieu*, Avenel, ed., Paris, 1863, Vol. III, pp. 179–213. The portions here translated appear on pages 179–183, 186, and 192–195 of the *Lettres*. Translated for this book by William F. Church. *Mémoires* published under the sponsorship of the Sociéré de l'histoire de France by Librairie Ancienne Honoré Champion, Paris. *Lettres* published by the Imprimerie Impériale (under government sponsorship).

Now that La Rochelle is taken, if the king wishes to make himself the most powerful monarch on earth and the most esteemed of princes, he should consider before God and carefully and secretly examine with his faithful servants what personal qualities are required of him and what should be reformed in his state.

The operation of the divine grace that was owed to God's bounty for such a success not only incites but compels me to make this proposal to your majesty and, to my mind, obliges you to embrace and follow it.

The interests of your state are divided into two parts, one concerning internal affairs, the other external.

Regarding the first, you must above all complete the destruction of the rebellion of heresy, take Castres, Nîmes, Montauban, and all remaining strongholds in Languedoc, Rouergue, and Guyenne. . . .

You must raze all strongholds that are not on the frontiers, do not protect crossings over rivers, or do not serve to curb rebellious and troublesome large cities. You must thoroughly fortify those on the frontiers, especially one at Commercy[1] which must be acquired. Lessen the burden on the lower classes. Discontinue the *paulette* when it terminates a year hence. Reduce and restrict those bodies [for example, the parlements] which, because of pretensions to sovereignty, always oppose the good of the realm. Ensure that your majesty is absolutely obeyed by great and small. Fill the bishoprics with carefully selected, wise, and capable men. Repurchase the royal domain and increase your revenue by one half, as far as may be done by harmless measures. . . .

In foreign affairs, you must have a continuing plan to stop the advance of Spain. Although that nation's objective is to increase its dominion and extend its boundaries, France should seek only to strengthen herself internally and to build and open gateways [on her borders] in order to be able to enter into the states of her neighbors and protect them from Spanish oppression when the occasion arises.

To that end, the first thing you must do is to make yourself

---

[1] A small town on the left bank of the Meuse, about thirty miles south of Verdun. (Editor's note.)

powerful on the sea which provides entry into all the states of the world.

Subsequently you must consider fortifying your position at Metz and advancing as far as Strasbourg if possible so as to gain a gateway into Germany. This must be done with great discretion and with quiet and clandestine methods.

You must build a great citadel at Versoix[2] to overawe the Swiss, have an open door into that country, and put Geneva in the position of being one of the outworks of France. . . .

You must consider [taking] the Marquisate of Saluzzo,[3] either through an understanding with the Duke of Savoy by giving him greater conquests in Italy if his mercurial disposition causes him to return to your majesty's service, or by taking advantage of the bad relations between him and the subjects of the Marquisate to reconquer it. . . .

In order to be in a position to be more respected as powerful in Italy, it is necessary to maintain thirty galleys and assign command of them by commission, revocable every three years, so that each commander will strive to call attention to his efforts and will not remain in port for his own benefit, as they have done until now, to the discredit of France.

We may think of Navarre and the Franche-Comté as belonging to us, since they are contiguous to France and easy to conquer whenever we have nothing else to do. This, however, should not be bruited about since it would be imprudent to consider it if these more important matters have not succeeded and because it could not be done without causing open war with Spain, which must be avoided as far as possible.

As for the person of the king, he has so many good qualities that it is difficult to find any to criticize. But since the sins of kings consist principally of omissions, it would not be surprising if there were something of this sort to note, not because he lacks the necessary princely attributes but because he fails to put them into practice.

A prince should permit his familiars to warn him of his shortcomings. . . .

[2] A small town on the western shore of Lake Geneva. (Editor's note.)
[3] A small piece of territory on the French border next to the Duchy of Savoy. (Editor's note.)

Your majesty should avoid like the plague a certain jealousy that often renders princes unable to tolerate their servants doing for them many things that are wholly necessary but which they do not wish or cannot do themselves. Otherwise there would be no one, no matter how well intentioned, who would dare exert himself to the full. This is dangerous because there are many occasions when it is impossible to remedy evils by temperate and moderate means whereas it is easy to do so by strong and powerful ones. Apprehension [of royal disapproval] prevents their being tried, since there are few men who are willing to assume the risk of incurring the indignation of their master for having served him too well.

In this regard, it must be frankly stated that either your majesty must determine to attend to your affairs with both diligence and authority, or you must comprehensively authorize someone else to handle them in this manner. Otherwise you will never be served and your affairs will be lost. . . .

It is so dangerous in a state to act indifferently in enforcing the laws that it is impossible for me not to observe that your majesty seems to show insufficient zeal and determination in enforcing yours, particularly the edict against duels. One may truly say that your majesty and your council will answer for all the souls that will be lost by this diabolical practice, since you might have prevented this by the rigorous punishments that such crimes deserve.

Nothing is more widespread than committing crimes in matters of state, disobeying a command of the king, and interfering with the execution of his edicts. Until recently, such disorders were committed with impunity, even though offenses of this nature are of such consequence, because of the examples and the results that they produce, that unless one is extraordinarily severe in punishing them, the state cannot survive.

The sins of kings as kings differ from those that they commit as mere men. As men, they are subject to all that God imposes upon human beings, but as kings they are bound to use their power strictly for the purposes for which they received it from heaven and, moreover, without abusing it by extending their rule beyond the limits prescribed for them.

Kings who use their power to despoil or oppress those who are inferior to them in strength, with no right but that of arms, condemn themselves by abusive and excessive extension of their power. Those who fail to use their authority to subject their states to the rule under which they belong are as guilty before God because of neglecting what they should do as are the others for committing what they may not legitimately do.

If a king permits his powerful subjects to oppress the weak with exactions and violence and remain unpunished, disrupting the tranquillity of the state that he is obliged to preserve as far as he can, he unquestionably destroys himself. Although as a man he may seem a saint, he will nevertheless be condemned as king. . . .

The king may pardon the disobedience of one of his subjects, but if he foresees that the recipient of the pardon may abuse it by bolder disobedience in the future, and if he fears that overlooking the offense may cause others to disobey and follow this example, disrupting peace in the state, he is bound to punish the crime and may not fail to do so without committing a greater one.

If your majesty will apply these general principles to specific occasions as they arise, you will protect yourself from many troubles that may bring great hurt to your state and to your conscience.

A Christian may not forgive an insult or pardon an offense too quickly, nor a king, governor, or magistrate punish them quickly enough when the crimes concern the state. This distinction is crucial, but the reason for it is clear and is based upon a single principle.

God did not leave punishment in the hands of individuals because, with this pretext, any man might follow his passions and disturb the public peace. On the contrary, He placed punishment in the hands of kings and magistrates according to the rules that He prescribed for them because, if [salutary] examples and penalties were lacking, any injustice and violence might be committed with impunity against the public tranquillity.

Men's salvation occurs ultimately in the next world, and it is therefore not surprising that God wishes men to leave to Him the punishment of the wrongs that He scourges with his judgments in eternity. But states have no being after this world. Their salvation is either in the present or nonexistent. Hence the punishments that are necessary to their survival may not be postponed but must be immediate.

Besides, justice must be rendered without passion. A prince

who exercises it while exempting some persons, hotly pursuing those who are disagreeable to him but excusing those who are so fortunate as to be in his good graces, must render an account of this to the tribunal of divine justice, which is higher than his own.

2   *Guez de Balzac*
The Ideal Prince

Jean-Louis de Guez, seigneur de Balzac (1594-1654), is best known as a rhetorician who contributed to the formation of the modern French language. He was also a partisan of Cardinal Richelieu and wrote in his support, but never succeeded in winning extensive favors from him. Balzac's most important political tract, Le Prince, *was first published in 1631 and is in the form of a panegyric of Louis XIII, but he clearly had in mind Richelieu's policies and strengthening of the monarchy. Although the work is written in a very stilted manner, it presents the major justification of absolutism during Richelieu's tenure of power—the restoration of a relative degree of order by the monarchy after the chaos and destruction of the Wars of Religion. Because of Balzac's extreme gratitude for this change, a sentiment felt by many of his contemporaries, he was moved to vindicate almost any actions that the ruler might take against recalcitrant subjects. Being an able logician, Balzac realized the implications of his position and did not hesitate to accept the rationality of reason of state, thereby justifying many of Richelieu's arbitrary measures.*

Knowing that our religion requires us to abstain from all appearance of evil and to do good not only before God but among men, our king is not content with hidden piety and mere spiritual

SOURCE. Jean-Louis de Guez de Balzac, *Le Prince*, in *Oeuvres*, Paris, 1854, Vol. I, pp. 50–52, 78–81, 84–86, 88–91, 93–95, 97–99. Translated for this book by William F. Church. Published in 1854 by Jacques Lecoffre et Cie., Paris.

adoration. He feels obliged to show his faith in public and to be
an example for the edification of his people. The smallest ceremonies that concern divine worship are reverenced by him. He
occasionally adds his voice to public prayers. . . . But since his
piety would be useless if it remained only in the highest realms
of intelligence, apart from affections and desires, he causes it to
descend from his head to his heart and from light to become
fire so that his high and noble understanding, so fertile in great
and admirable effects, will not be limited to the idle pleasures
of meditation.

Therefore, let us not regard his religion as mere peaceful,
untroubled worship before the altar, for it is found as well in
war. It appears at the head of his troops and in the trenches; it
exposes the most precious life on earth today to all the perils of
fortune. . . . It is needful that a prince be devout in this fashion,
as our king was at the battle on the Ile de Ré and at the defeat
of the English. He was incapable of performing a more pious act,
and if it was inferior to those of the martyrs, which I find difficult to admit, it was so only by one degree since in Christian
humility suffering is prized more than the causing of it. . . .

For ten years he has watched over us and has been almost
constantly on horseback, travelling wherever public necessity
calls him. Although he well knows that kings and realms may not
enjoy the same repose, he is content to assume the difficulties
and dangers to himself and to leave peace and security to France.
His white hair has resulted from the noble and glorious anxiety
that has brought tranquillity to his people. Every winter the rain
and snow beat down on the first head in the world. In the greatest
heat of the summer, when we use all possible means to keep cool
and find shade, his face is burned by the sun of Languedoc, usually
in the open field ten days' journey from the Louvre, subject to
injury from air and season. Some of his predecessors found it
more difficult to bestir themselves and move from their quarters
to the council chamber than he does in going from one end of
the realm to the other. He makes his inspections from Paris to
Guyenne and Dauphiné, and there is no afflicted area of his
state whose wounds and ills do not immediately feel the relief
that his presence brings wherever he shows himself. . . .

Let us not speak ungratefully of our prosperity. Let us not

contradict public sentiment. Let us not weaken the truth by malicious exceptions and limited praise. Let us at least confess our obligations to the king even though we cannot comprehend them. There never was a ruler so well-disposed to do right as urged by political philosophers; never were there greater promises for the future. We no longer fear the ruin of our state; we have unending hope. All parts of this superb body that was wracked so long are again strengthened. Everything is encompassed by an admirable justice; hardly a stone is out of place; nothing offends our sensibilities. For the first time slander is nowhere to be heard. There are no faults to uncover and almost no wishes to make.

I can hardly believe my own eyes and impressions when I consider the present and recall the past. It is no longer the France that recently was so torn apart, ill and decrepit. No longer are the French enemies of their country, slothful in the service of their prince and despised by other nations. Behind their faces I see other men and in the same realm another state. The form remains, but the interior has been renewed. There has occurred a moral revolution, a change of spirit, a most agreeable progress from evil to good. The king has restored the good repute of his subjects, communicated his strength and vigor to the state, and corrected the faults of the previous century; he has eliminated both indolence and recklessness from public affairs. . . .

Besides, only a civil war is needed to break up the state and destroy monarchical government. What else did we see but civil wars after the death of Henry II? And were they not so frequent that we could count the years by the peace treaties that had to be made? Our kings signed their death warrant or at least their deposition when they joined the Catholic League and, of the two factions that were destroying the realm, they gave the League their arms and authority in order to remain unarmed and unprotected against the attacks of both. If they had been guided by reason, they would never have made such a mistake, and if royal prudence had existed at that time, there would have been neither League nor Huguenots. The latter, which should have been crushed in infancy and might easily have been routed, grew because of the sovereign's indulgence, found their initial strength in contempt for their weakness, and finally grew to

such great size that they often equalled royal power. Their ruin
has been the masterpiece of Louis the Just.

But before this courageous prince came into the world to save
us and put things in their proper order, how many times did
these two rebellious factions nearly succeed? How close did we
come to having a Republic of Languedoc, Estates of Guyenne,
Dukes of Burgundy and Counts of Provence? And who could
tell our fathers that the rebellion would finally exhaust itself
against one who alone was capable of destroying it? . . .

Among us, proper punishments and rewards have almost never
been known. The great have always offended the small with
impunity, and the weak have always been the prey of the powerful. . . . They not only go unpunished but receive rewards. They
have been carefully sought after and given all sorts of favors.
They have always gained by doing evil and have profited from
their faults. . . .

Might not these and similar disorders destroy France? Have
not many states perished because of less? . . . Chance alone has
saved us, or to speak in a more Christian manner and avoid corrupt, pagan terms, it is God that took particular care of deserted
France and became her guardian in her trials. It is his providence
that continually combats the imprudence of men and heaven
that matches their faults with as many miracles. . . . But in our
present condition, we can easily withstand the storm and dispense with this extraordinary assistance on which we cannot
always rely. . . .

The light of our king's mind appears chiefly in his policies.
To do extraordinary things, it is not sufficient to know how to
make use of one's time; one must recognize the appropriate
moment. Civil prudence no less than knowledge of justice takes
account of good and bad hours as suited to deeds or repose. All
human actions have their right moment, for even the most vir-
tuous may be done inopportunely. . . . Men do not create opportunities but are given them; they do not order time but possess
only a small part of it, the present, which is but an almost im-
perceptible point as opposed to the vast extent of the limitless
future. To achieve their ends, men must move quickly and in
good time; they must make haste among immediate, transitory
things. In addition to the understanding that our wise prince

has gained from his experience and his reason, he is enlightened by God, for he said, speaking of himself, that he had been killing the wicked ever since morning and was apparently uncertain of the afternoon, since he did not know whether his good fortune would last that long.

These maxims are necessary at the height of a storm and in great extremities, but they are also useful when one perceives some sign of change or the least symptom of disorder. The king therefore does not abandon them in such instances, even though in calm, peaceful times he follows others that are more pleasant and humane. He sometimes has opposed his ready strength to incipient violence. He has waged small wars to avoid great ones. He has perhaps sacrificed two or three heads in order to reestablish public tranquillity, for his clemency has not always overcome his justice. . . .

The king who brings himself to use forceful remedies only with difficulty has occasionally made use of milder ones. He has discovered that excellent mean between punishment and pardon, between rigor and indulgence. To tell the truth, it seems to me quite reasonable to take action in advance of certain crimes that cannot be punished after they are committed and not to defer remedying the evil until the criminals have made themselves masters of their judges. It is true that because of foolish pity we always favor those who rebel against princes, since the more powerful party is always regarded as the more offensive and harm is assumed to stem from strength rather than weakness. The people will not believe that a conspiracy against the king has occurred until he is dead. However, I do not advise rulers to allow themselves to be killed in order to demonstrate the validity of this distrust of them nor to fall into traps that are set for them so as to prove that they have no reason to fear. They may forestall the danger even by executing those whom they suspect; it is an excusable severity. But it is also a mark of clemency, most appropriate to kings and impossible to praise sufficiently, to accomplish the same end without executing anyone.

Upon a mere suspicion, a minor misgiving, a dream that he may have had, why should not the prince be permitted to make sure of his rebellious subjects and put his mind at ease by punishing them merely with their own safety? Why should not a faithful servant joyfully suffer detention that would demonstrate his fidelity, contradict the calumny of his accusers, and appease the anxiety of his master?

Is it not better to prevent crimes by the innocent than to be reduced to the sad necessity of punishing the guilty? Are not acts of this type exercises in clemency? Do they not usually result in the preservation of persons who would otherwise ruin themselves? If such simple means were used to combat the evils that menace the state, the liberty of a single individual would not so frequently ruin entire realms. If the instigators of our rebellions had been quickly seized, not only would they have been saved but an infinite number of other lives would have been spared as well as all the blood that was spilled during the civil wars. If the bad winds had been stopped, the sea would not have become agitated; if kings had enough prudence, they would have little use for justice.

I mean that punctilious and scrupulous justice that will not condemn crimes that are afoot because they have not yet been committed, that waits until the rebels have ruined the state before it may legitimately move against them, and that observes the letter of the law but allows all laws to perish. This highest equity is supreme injustice, and it would be a sin against reason in this instance not to sin against the forms. . . . Prudence must modify justice in many things. Justice without prudence would move too slowly and never be complete, and prudence must prevent crimes whose punishment would be either impossible or dangerous. Justice is rendered only according to the actions of men, but prudence has authority over their thoughts and secrets. It extends into the future; it concerns the general welfare; it provides for the good of posterity. And for these reasons it must everywhere make use of means that the laws do not ordain but necessity justifies, and that would not be entirely good if they were not for a good end.

Public utility often benefits from injury to individuals. . . . We should willingly endure brief pain that brings long prosperity. We may not honorably seek relief from a burden that we share with our master, and when the prince puts forth great effort and does not spare himself, it is fitting that the subjects assume their part and that no one in the realm remain indolent or cowardly while he labors and risks his life.

3   *Mathieu de Morgues*
            Appeal to the King

Mathieu de Morgues (1582–1670) was a very able pamphleteer during the reign of Louis XIII and was the most indefatigable of Richelieu's many critics. Early in his career, Morgues was closely associated with the Cardinal and wrote in his support, but after the definitive break between Louis XIII and Marie de Medici in 1631, Morgues joined the latter in the Low Countries and produced a steady stream of pamphlets in which he criticized all aspects of Richelieu's policies. That his knowledge of them was thorough is attested by the remarkable fullness of his information regarding major developments. The majority of his writings were in defense of Marie de Medici and, to a lesser extent, Gaston d'Orléans, but he occasionally considered broader matters as in the present selection. His appeal to Louis XIII to cast off Richelieu and return to a more traditional type of government reveals the nature of much of the resentment against Richelieu's "rule." It also indicates that the Cardinal's critics were helpless to alter royal policy as long as Louis XIII gave Richelieu his full support.

Sire, all the fine qualities that we observe in your majesty, in the Queen Mother, and in Monsieur, your only brother, greatly contribute to the felicity of your reign, the preservation of peace in your realm, the relief of your subjects, and good relations

SOURCE. Mathieu de Morgues, *Très humble, très véritable et très importante Remontrance au Roi*, n.p., 1631. Reprinted in Morgues, *Diverses Pièces pour la défense de la Reine Mère du Roi très chrétien, Louis XIII*, n.p., 1637, Vol. I, where the portions here translated appear on pages 3, 6–8, 38–39, 42–44, 77–79, 100, 102. Translated for this book by William F. Church.

with your allies and neighbors. We expected all these benefits
from the concurrence of such admirable moral and Christian vir-
tues. We may truly say that we were confirmed in this hope
when, at the Queen Mother's request, it pleased you to bring
Cardinal Richelieu into your council. Many persons knew him
to be a man of subtle mind, not easily surprised because always
on guard, a man who sleeps little and works much, considers
everything, is skillful, speaks well, and is reasonably informed
on foreign affairs. When this choice was made, it was thought
that his great desire for honor and glory would cause him to
do good and avoid evil. . . .

Alas, Sire, what have we seen during the time that you have
enjoyed such fine qualities and he who receives all praise has
been your chief minister? We have seen the realm afflicted by
war, pestilence, and famine; the three scourges of God have joined
together to plague us. God has shown us that there is something
not only in our personal morality but our collective conduct that
displeases his divine Majesty, causing Him to call down on us all
the maledictions that He unleashes in his anger on his people.
There are provinces of France where only a third of the inhabitants who lived there three years ago remain. It is said that pestilence and famine are among the ills that flow from God and
that men's prudence and charity may neither prevent nor cure
them because they arise from the evil influences of the air and
the earth, but your majesty well knows those who, instead of
arresting these disorders, have caused you daily to lose thereby
as many men as would die in a battle. At the same time and for
the same reasons, we see five or six of the most important frontier
provinces of your realm greatly disrupted by changes that have
been introduced. For six years, they have suffered from the passage of troops and extraordinary levies of money, beasts of burdens, grain and other supplies. Disease has almost depopulated
these areas and rendered their fields sterile; hunger has caused
men to eat the animals needed for cultivating the soil. To this
has been added the discontent of all officers of justice who are
mulcted like money lenders, causing them to lose not only your
people's respect but the authority to keep them in order. All
things are thus reduced to force and the necessity of preserving
obedience in the cities and coercing them to accept these innova-

tions. All this where once there was merely love and quiet, effective justice that armies cannot maintain when they are quartered among families whose greatest enemies are unpaid soldiers.

At the same time, we hear ecclesiastics say that a single man [Richelieu] possesses twenty abbeys and extracts his taxes from the poor priests. The nobility complain that he brings lawsuits against privileged persons and officers of the crown like any commoners, that their honor and lives depend on the corruption of some agent with only a smattering of knowledge, that marshals of France are imprisoned without cause and denied the formalities of justice, and that the rewards that gentlemen might hope to receive for their services are reserved for those who have the Cardinal's confidence and are used to further his aims. Captains and soldiers alike are in despair at being reduced to begging, while mere guards who are always sheltered receive handsome rewards. . . . No troops are well paid but those who guard the many maritime emplacements, the only well-provisioned ones, that serve as havens for the treasure and the person of the man who has persuaded your majesty that nothing is secure unless confided to him. He spends more on these garrisons than on the subsistence of an army of twenty thousand men. Officeholders, merchants, and the poor people say that he takes their last *écu* without your majesty becoming the richer; although your gifts, expenses, and payments are reduced by a third, your pleasures are limited, your delights cost you nothing, your buildings are very few, and your armies desert for lack of wages. . . .

When ambition, Sire, attains its highest goals, it changes into presumption, audacity, boldness, cruelty, and tyranny. These are the weapons with which it defends itself and attacks all that threaten or appear to oppose it. It takes pleasure in causing its power to be felt by the greatest and in frightening the humble. Fearing everyone, it causes itself to be universally feared; neither capable nor desirous of inspiring love, it becomes terrifying to all. It surrounds itself with guards, not as a king but as a tyrant who fears the fruits of the despair that he inspires in everyone.

The ambitious have never taken this road in a free monarchy nor among a people accustomed to the comfort of a long-established and just rule. If the Cardinal persists in this policy many more years, all past experience must be deceptive and God must have abandoned not only the direction of your state but the protection of the innocent. . . .

Sire, you are the sovereign judge of all your people. God has given you the sword of justice as well as that of war. False witnesses, produced by those who control your affairs and report to you as counsel before a court, are those who now condemn men although you sometimes order their arrest. I say sometimes because I know that arrests and imprisonments are often made without your knowledge. If you are informed, evidence is falsified and favorable information suppressed. . . . In order to magnify matters of small importance, they allege the safety of your person and your state; they enter the formidable charge of leze majesty in the highest degree and say that your authority will be lost if those whom they wish to destroy are not condemned. If the sovereign courts remonstrate against edicts that oppress the people, if frontier provinces point to their privileges which your majesty has confirmed, and if they oppose the introduction of changes that will ruin them, all are reduced to questions of authority. Petitions are called rebellion; no mention is made of kindness, clemency, or justice—only severity, rigor, and force. No one points to the people's misery, the disorder caused by war, the ravages of disease, the extent of famine. . . . They try to persuade you that it is good policy to lose the hearts of men while preserving the body of your state, as if it could survive without that which gives it life and strength for your service. . . .

Our good kings, your predecessors, understood what all earlier political writers maintain and the histories of all the world's governments confirm, that monarchies untempered by aristocracy are of short duration because they first become suspect and then odious to the people who readily criticize them. Our kings wished to avoid both this reputation and its effect. They knew that the laws of their state and the submission of the French permit them to dispose of their subjects' lives and goods and even to create new taxes, offices, and regulations according to need. That these innovations might be more readily accepted according to justice, the kings voluntarily allowed them to be examined and verified by the sovereign courts, both to clear the kings' consciences before God and to preserve their reputation among men. They nonetheless reserved the right to use the absolute authority that is indicated by these words which they added to all letters patent and edicts, *tel est notre bon plaisir*. Good princes like you content themselves with writing these words on parchment to demonstrate their power, but they never make use of all their sovereign authority, which should be exercised with caution, preferably according to customary usage so that he who holds it may be loved and revered. Murmurs arise against a ruler who acts otherwise and criticisms of his government make their appearance, inclining men little by little to rebellion. Forgive me if I disclose this very important truth to you. I would not love your person nor your state if I were to hide it. . . .

It is most important that your majesty examine the aims of those who would undertake purposeless wars and refuse to terminate them with great advantage to your glory and benefit to your captains, soldiers, supplies, finances, and the poor people but continue them with general ruin so as to make themselves more necessary and avenge their personal quarrels. This is abominable before God and punishable under justice in all the states of the globe. Sire, good and wise kings undertake war only because of necessity and wage it solely to establish peace in their states or to gain it for their allies. When peace is proposed and the occasion arises for giving or accepting it without loss of reputation, one should embrace it like a daughter of God, sister of justice, mother of abundance, guardian of piety, and the most treasured gift that heaven may send to earth or kings may give their subjects. . . .

Sire, we do not doubt that your goodness and piety embody great compassion for the many poor Christians and Frenchmen that God has placed under your authority. They are the images of his mind as you are that of his power, but their misery is hidden from you. You are not told and cannot see the great number that have fled to foreign lands and have become soldiers of your enemies, how many you have lost through famine, the daughter of war and mother of pestilence, and what desolation these three scourges have brought many provinces. The oppressed and all others find hope only in your goodness, daily praying God for your prosperity and health, and asking holy Providence to give you a council composed of upright men who will second your good intentions for the relief of all and preserve your royal dignity whose support lies, as Solomon said, in the multitude of the people.

4   *Claude Joly*
True Maxims of Government

Claude Joly (1607–1700) was a member of a famous family of jurists and received excellent legal training early in his career. He was also attracted to the religious life, took orders, and wrote many treatises on religious subjects. The latter circumstance doubtless accounts for the strong moral tone of the work excerpted here. During the Fronde, Joly lent his considerable abilities to the support of the rebels by writing his famous Maximes véritables *which became the most important theoretical justification of the movement. In essence, Joly's argument was that Cardinal Mazarin and other flatterers at court had corrupted the government by causing the Regent to violate the traditions of the French monarchy. The King of France should rule within the limitations of legal tradition and Christian morality, sparing the lives and goods of his subjects and undertaking war only as a last resort. Above all, he should abide by the principles of Christianity, applying its precepts to his public policies as well as to his private life. Joly was convinced that only this type of government was tolerable in a Christian monarchy, and he understandably rejected the concept of reason of state which justified royal policy in very different terms. There was much in the French tradition to support this concept of limited monarchy, but Joly's appeal went unheeded and the failure of the* Fronde *merely had the result of strengthening royal absolutism.*

SOURCE. Claude Joly, *Recueil des maximes véritables et importantes pour l'institution du roi*, Paris, 1663, pp. i-viii, 18, 20–21, 26, 41–43, 51, 63–67, 130–131, 149–150, 156–158, 423–424, 427–428, 440, 445–446, 455–458, 538, 553–555. Translated for this book by William F. Church.

Someone has written that all good kings might easily be represented by the single portrait on a signet ring, but one of our historians remarks that all the bad kings of France might also be similarly represented. I am not surprised that this glorious exception is made of our kings, since they have the special honor of being called Most Christian and bear the title, Eldest Son of the Church.

But what greatly surprises me is to find that neither the religion of the most pious nor the kindness of the most merciful has prevented our experiencing the many ills that afflict the state. The excesses of the most recent rulers, which still plague us, have caused us to forget those of earlier rulers, but if we wish to refresh our memories we shall find the latter's excesses were also very great.

From whence come such frequent troubles? And how is it that our kings' good natures have so frequently been fruitless and have not brought the relief that we should have received? It is because at the same time that their inclinations favor the good of their subjects, they are diverted by the malice of their favorites and ministers who have too much influence over their minds and blind them, so to speak, causing them to believe that evil is good. Because of this, they authorize great violence and injustice that benefit the ministers' personal interests and advantages but oppress the people. . . .

Although Cardinal Mazarin is incompetent in all things but the infamous art of deceit, it has not been difficult for him to imitate the earlier corruptors of princes who preceded him, since he found himself after the death of King Louis XIII (of glorious memory) in possession of the mind of the Queen, then Regent, and later that of her son, both because of her influence and the new title of superintendent of his majesty's education, which Mazarin gave himself in order to possess this young royal mind more easily. . . .

Although it seems that the principal reason for seeking the permanent banishment of this alien minister is our deliverance from our present ills, . . . nevertheless the greatest and most pressing reason . . . is our well-founded fear that this pernicious superintendent of our young monarch's education will in time pervert all his good inclinations toward virtue and the welfare and relief of his subjects. . . .

That is why it is most important to ensure that the corrupt doctrine that this bad preceptor has given the king will not penetrate his heart, the place from which come evil thoughts capable of raising tempests. For this purpose, it is most appropriate to inform his majesty of the truths that are contrary to the falsehoods with which he has been imbued so as to instruct him concerning what he may and should do, and still more what he may not and should not do. . . .

The power of kings is not absolute and without limits. And since it is important to instruct them, . . . it is necessary to begin by establishing this maxim that carries with it many others, for example, that the power of kings is bounded and limited, and that they may not dispose of their subjects according to their will and pleasure. . . .

However, the flattery of courtiers has advanced to such a degree of audacity and extravagance that some impertinent men attempt to persuade kings that they may rightfully dispose of their subjects' lives and goods at will. . . . This pretended right is a weak foundation for the absolute and tyrannical power with which ministers and courtiers delude the king in order to solidify their positions and subject the people to a blind obedience that would be greater than that which we give to God who demands from us only a reasonable obedience, according to the Apostle. . . .

Who is not astonished by the flood of ills that we have suffered for several years and the great number of crimes that are daily committed by undisciplined soldiers, even though the Queen, who controls matters of state and cannot be ignorant of all the remonstrances that have been presented to her by courts, cities, communities, and individuals, converses with many pious persons, enters retreats with nuns in their cells, frequents the holy sacraments of the Church, and remains attached to religion?

From whence comes all of this if not from the hypocrisy that is used to convince the Queen that evil is not evil and from the criminal flattery with which her innocence is deceived? Should we not assume that her conscience would cause her to terminate these ills if she were not betrayed by the infamous complacency of those who surround her? And is there not good reason to believe rumors that wicked deceivers have convinced her that in all she has done to maintain Cardinal Mazarin in power, she has not committed a single venial sin? And that consequently she has not participated in any of the carnage, fire, ravishing, and sacrilege that have been perpetrated for three years by the French, German, and Polish troops that this miserable minister has used in the name and authority of the king? It is as though . . . those who govern and hold power are not responsible before the throne of the divine Majesty for all the evils that are committed by their followers insofar as they have knowledge of these matters. . . .

It seems from all of this that we may not judge rulers by external evidences of their devotion but rather by their sincerity and the excellence of the deeds with which they worthily acquit themselves of the commission that God gave them. They must believe that since faith without works is dead, each man is required to exercise his faith according to his calling. The faith of princes is vain and useless if they do not cultivate it by the acts to which they are obligated by their titles, principally the rendering of justice to their subjects and constantly caring for their safety and protection. . . .

Moreover, it is a very great error, against which kings should be warned, that politics and Christian piety are incompatible and that it is impossible to accommodate the laws of the state to those of the Gospel. This most dangerous opinion is sometimes insinuated into their minds and not only does great damage to their consciences but is particularly detrimental to a King of France because it may cause him to do many things that would completely tarnish his beautiful name of Most Christian.

I can hardly endure the words of one of our foremost magistrates who, when attending the king in the Parlement at the registration of some edicts, . . . was asked his advice and answered . . . that there is one conscience for affairs of state and another for personal matters.

These accursed maxims have circulated among the greatest jurists today and have rendered them pliable to all the desires of royal favorites. This is a major cause of the ills that we suffer, since the ministers' injustice and oppression of the people for twenty or thirty years, in the name of the king whose authority they usurp, have occurred with the assistance of these officials. . . . From this have come all the uprisings that have violently agitated this state in recent years and are capable of destroying it if no decision is made to govern the people with greater justice and kindness than in the past.

Now I say that the maxim concerning the incompatability of religion and politics is entirely false and cannot be true except for those who seek to govern tyrannically. . . .

The pagans never dreamed of the rules and precepts that Jesus Christ taught and prescribed for us, yet one cannot find in any work of their most celebrated authors who wrote on political matters any maxims contrary to the laws of Christianity. In all Cicero, who understood both the practical and speculative art of government and guided Rome's affairs during the most difficult times of the Republic, as he says, we will not find a single maxim that does not easily accord with those of our Gospel. . . .

Certain persons who are badly informed concerning the rights of the sovereign believe that the people were made for kings, whereas on the contrary it is true that kings were made only for the people. There have always been people without kings, but never kings without people.

Because of this, and because the people cannot live without justice, it is entirely correct to say that kings were created to render justice to their people. It was owing to their need of justice that the people resolved to erect a king over themselves. . . .

From this, it should not be difficult to prove that kings are bound by law, for that which does not conform to approved and accepted law may not be regarded as just. . . . Those who seek to ascribe power to the Kings of France comparable to that which the Roman Emperors attributed to themselves sometimes make use of the rule or proverb, *Qui veut le Roy si veut la Loy*,[1] as though this means that the law is nothing but the will of the sovereign. But it is much more natural to interpret

---

[1] As the king wills, so wills the law. This is the first legal maxim in Antoine Loisel, *Institutes coutumières*, Paris, 1607. (Editor's note.)

this as *Qui veut le Roy veut aussi la Loy*,[2] . . . because it seems that the people never intended to submit purely and simply, without reservation, to the king's discretion but only on condition that he govern according to the rule of law. It is a reciprocal contract that is formed of two equal parts, the proposal that one party makes and the free acceptance of it by the other. It follows that the king is not absolute master of the law and may not ruin and destroy it whenever he pleases, since by the contract the people submitted to him only on condition that he preserve and maintain the law. . . .

It is a dangerous falsehood, which avaricious ministers and ambitious persons have sought to insinuate into the minds of kings, that they are absolute masters of the lives and goods of their subjects and that, consequently, all that belongs to us is theirs to take and distribute to others at will whenever they please.

Now, I entirely disapprove of calling the king our master unless we understand this to be a mere figure of speech, implying nothing that is not intended by the word "king." I myself have used the term "master" in this sense in this book, indicating the profound respect and veneration that I owe royal majesty. But when it is a question of proper and exact terms, I say that the word "master" is the diametrical opposite of "king." For persons who are completely different from a master, such as slaves or domestics, are made for the master, . . . but it is the king who is made for his subjects. . . .

From this it follows that if kings, speaking strictly and not in terms of respect and honor, cannot be called our masters, it is impossible to urge the untenable proposition that they are masters of our lives and goods. On the contrary, we must conclude with all assurance that since they are not masters of our goods, they have no right to take them nor to levy taxes from us without our will and consent. . . .

Not only was it formerly necessary to obtain the consent of the Estates General to levies in France, but we also know that the Estates General had the right to name commissioners for the execution of their decisions. . . .

---

[2] As the king wills, the law also wills. That is, the king's will does not contravene the law. (Editor's note.)

If it is a crime for a king to levy taxes from the people without their consent, what should we call the measures that are done in his name by his favorites and ministers who ruin whole provinces with endless taxes and reduce so many poor officials, bourgeois, and peasants to mendicity in order to gorge themselves with wealth, raise themselves to titles of dukes and peers, and do many other things that are entirely above their birth and merit? . . .

The ideas of Erasmus would be very appropriate to teach a young king, for he would then be shown the blindness in which princes are kept so as to make them believe that they acquire great glory and properly conduct their affairs when they risk losing their states through the hazards of war or at least cause the deaths and ruin of a great many of their subjects, instead of putting them at ease and ruling them in a firm and durable peace. All this, merely to ruin a province of a neighboring prince by means as unchristian as they are cruel and to take three or four wretched cities that cost more to keep than they are worth and whose wealth goes merely to some governors who pillage the people. . . . Experience shows that, since the King of France is too powerful to be ruined by the King of Spain and vice versa, wars result from the bad counsel that both rulers receive from their ministers, who merely wish to create confusion in order to find excuses to wring taxes from the people, keep the great nobles away from court in order to be absolute masters there, cause many quick deaths so as to have many offices to fill, and rid themselves of those whom they dislike. . . .

Thus it is folly for a prince to make war except in great necessity and after having tried all possible means of preserving peace, even under disadvantageous conditions, for the maxim that we teach—that even an unjust peace is better than war—is not a trivial or vulgar saying. . . .

It is God who punishes bad kings and punishes them most rigorously; very rarely does He neglect to punish them in this world. . . . Princes should be taught that they have a great obligation to God. He may punish them in this world, using this temporal punishment to lessen the eternal punishment, which is more severe for kings and princes than for others.

I have occasionally reflected on the words of the Son of God where He teaches us that when He comes in his majesty at the day of the last judgment, He will admit to his Father's realm only those who have performed acts of mercy toward the poor, to whom He seems principally to attach the salvation of all men, and will condemn to eternal flames those who have neglected the poor. And I have thought that by this teaching, He attributes the cause of damnation to a single sin of omission.

This passage of Scripture is truly capable of astonishing everyone, but it should particularly cause kings to tremble in terror as well as all who have the power to do good or evil. For if it is true that God punishes so rigorously those who have failed to make use of their resources to aid the poor, how horrible will be the hell and punishment of princes who, because of bad conduct, nonchalance, uncontrolled passion, concern for small matters of honor, or unfounded authority . . . levy taxes and wage cruel, barbarous wars with which they ruin their people, reducing them from riches to poverty and to inconceivable need and misery?

COMMENTARIES

5   *Victor L. Tapié*
                The Legacy of Richelieu

Victor-Lucien Tapié, Professor at the Faculty of Letters in Paris and member of the Institute, has published a number of very valuable books and articles on the history and cultural growth of Europe during the early modern period and is an outstanding authority in the field. His volume that is excerpted here is generally regarded as the best treatment of France during the reign of Louis XIII to be published in recent years. Combining thorough scholarship with sound interpretations, it expertly synthesizes known information, presents important views on all major disputed topics, and may be consulted with profit concerning almost any aspect of the period. The conclusion of the book, which is presented here, embodies the most widely accepted view of the significance of Cardinal Richelieu's contribution to the growth of France.

Louis XIII and Richelieu lay, one in the crypt at Saint-Denis and the other under the dome of the Sorbonne, those two great actors who left behind them not an empty stage but one given over to lesser figures. In the realm, only the hope of peace was sufficient to compensate for the excessive nature of the effort that had been required and exceeded the resources of the nation.

SOURCE. Victor L. Tapié, *La France de Louis XIII et de Richelieu*, Paris: Librairie Flammarion, 1967 edition, pp. 403–409, 411–413. Translated for this book by William F. Church. Reprinted by permission of Macmillan & Co. Ltd. who will publish an English version translated by David Lockie. Copyright 1967 by Flammarion.

Extension of the war and the expenses that it entailed had compromised and arrested the program of relief and reconstruction that Richelieu had judged indispensable during the first part of his ministry sixteen years earlier; moreover it had caused further calamities. France was therefore wretched, the majority of Frenchmen in financial straits and harrassed. It would be fruitless to ask whether these troubles were worse than those of 1610 or 1620, for the evaluation of public and private ills is very relative and depends, as we say today, on the degree to which those concerned are capable of understanding their misery.

It is certain, however, that this exhausted and discontented France was a much stronger state in the Europe and the world of her time, was endowed with greater resources, more respected and formidable than the disordered realm of 1624, and that French society possessed a more extensive elite that adhered to political, moral, and intellectual values of a higher order.

Should the credit for this progress be ascribed to the government that had directed it? The government had evolved toward absolutism, that is, in all areas the authority of the king and those who acted under his orders—and no longer merely in his name, as formerly—had been strengthened at the expense of privileges that until then had guaranteed the liberty of individuals and groups. It seems certain that there were fewer liberties in the realm. But for this juxtaposition of liberties, which were foreign to each other and sometimes contradictory, was now substituted a union of all in a common work, the good of the state. It must be remembered that these liberties, which were based on tradition and privilege and chiefly benefited certain small groups, keeping them in a stagnant condition without horizon or means of developing and making use of their resources, bore no resemblance to the liberty of man as it was later conceived and gave every individual access to an improved situation in which he was assured of a better lot and might acquire greater understanding of his destiny. By involving the entire nation in the service of the king and a stronger state, the absolutism of Louis XIII and Richelieu, in a sense, released France from her medieval limitations and opened wider perspectives for all Frenchmen.

For we must not hold to illusions. The France of the Regency and the first years of Louis XIII, having replaced the France that Henry IV had restored, was an object of prey. In 1643, any lay or ecclesiastical lord, member of the Parlement, financial officer, trader, or shipowner in the ports might regret the passing of earlier years when interference by royal power seemed less heavy, when his daily activity practically escaped control, and when his profits seemed better guaranteed. And what may be said of the peasant, the mainspring but also the beast of burden of the entire system? But would they have gained very much by remaining the subjects of a weakened realm and a paralyzed government?

Several provinces of France were still in dispute. The House of Austria had not forgotten its long-standing claims to Burgundy, and Calais had only recently been freed from England. The reunion of Brittany with the crown was hardly a century old. French titles to Metz, Toul, and Verdun had not been ratified. It was Henry IV who had brought Béarn back into the French community and strengthened the strategic position of Lyon by acquiring Bresse and Bugey. There is much to warrant the assumption that such a France, divided by factions, would sooner or later in one way or another have been involved in a European war, once more invaded and subjected to dismemberment.

Without venturing arguments drawn from suppositions and events that did not happen, we cannot forget that the French navy was nonexistent in 1610 and that from the viewpoint of economics France paid tribute to Dutch, Spanish, and English merchant vessels and was even blockaded. In the final analysis, it is impossible to deny that if France had been left to her own devices and her people given over to their habits, which were far from peaceable, more and more she would have become a vassal state whose inhabitants worked for the benefit of foreigners. It would be folly and nonsense to imagine that neighboring states and their subjects would have respected the borders of this inviting land and refused to disrupt her apathy and domestic quarrels. To be or not to be, that was the question for our country. Louis XIII and Richelieu chose to be.

We certainly do not find evidence of a very high level of international morality (although the conditions at the time were such) if we must admit that a state was strong only on condition of having weak neighbors. The good fortune of our land was the constant weakening of Germany, its depopulation in the drama of incessant war on its territory, the economic crisis that checked the relative prosperity of Spain, and the internal quarrels in England. It would be odious and absurd in this instance to claim to deduce pseudolessons from history and urge that a perpetual and irrevocable rule links the greatness of our country with the misfortunes of our neighbors, making the latter a condition of the former. The divisions of a Europe that might have found within herself so many reasons for union and solidarity, and the necessity of war that brought so many misfortunes and so much destruction even to those who waged it successfully—these were the terrible defects of the seventeenth century, so attractive in many other qualities, and are surely the characteristics that were most repugnant to the Christian conscience as well as the ideal of classic reason. But we must emphasize the little word used earlier: *then*, the conditions of *then* alone count for the historian's explanations. Now, no state was *then* powerful or rich enough to establish about itself the combination of peace and economic progress, but a resolute state might safeguard the conditions that were necessary to its territorial independence and cause its natural resources to bear fruit. The merit of Richelieu seems to lie here, as that of Louis XIII in realizing that his minister served him well.

Let us examine the results. France in 1643 extended much further than in 1610. She reached beyond the valley of the Somme to the plateau of Artois where she controlled the principal cities; she dominated Lorraine and Alsace, Metz, Nancy, Colmar, and the bridges of the upper Rhine; she had a foothold in Italy, occupied Roussillon, and protected Catalonia. Through an alliance with Portugal, she wielded influence in the Iberian Peninsula. Her rebuilt navy permitted her to trade in the Mediterranean, the Atlantic, and the northern seas. She had colonies in Canada and the Antilles whose inhabitants, "descended from the French and even natives converted to the Christian faith and making profession of it were to be deemed and reputed natural French, capable of holding all offices, honors, inheritances and gifts without being required to obtain letters of naturalization."[1] She possessed settlements on the coast of Senegal and Madagascar. In less that twenty years she had become greater in the world than ever before.

Although Richelieu lacked the competence of an economist or financier, he had sufficiently broad intelligence to become interested in problems that another statesman in his place might easily have found reason to ignore. Louis XIII, attracted as a ruler by general ideas concerning monarchical authority, the unity of religious faith, and the nature of his private life, skilled in military matters and a lover of music, would doubtless not have been concerned with economic growth, certainly much less than his father, Henry IV, who at least had an interest in the matter as well as misgivings. The rare capacity of Richelieu's mind caused him to realize that France would be great not only because of the power that more extensive and better defended territory assured but by better utilization of her resources and skillful distribution of her merchandise throughout the world. Because of his acts, agrarian and feudal France began to participate in the commercial capitalism that was the new form of profitable economic activity of the time and had given the advantage to the Spanish, then the Dutch, and would soon establish the world greatness of England.

And it is clear (although war compromised this effort toward commercial development like all other efforts for recovery, but doubtless a little less because of the growth of the navy), that from 1624 to 1642 Richelieu attached major importance to this question because he cherished, as M. Hauser has observed, a "broad ideal of the national economy" and had the "future in his mind."[2]

---

[1] Article 13 of the Edict of Narbonne, March, 1642, renewing the privilege of the Company of the American Isles. Isambert, *et al.*, eds., *Recueil général des anciennes lois françaises*, Vol. XVI., Paris, n.d., p. 544.

[2] See H. Hauser, *La Pensée et l'action économiques du Cardinal de Richelieu*, Paris, 1944, the interesting pages of the conclusion on the role and ability of Richelieu as an economist as well as the comparison with Colbert, which is favorable to Richelieu with reason, it seems.

The social tragedy was that the advantages of this progress were not generally felt even in the time when it took place. A small number of individuals became wealthy, usually those who had already attained affluence and owned something that might be risked in such undertakings. Although great fortunes were created, they merely caused the distance between the traders, the immediate beneficiaries of the political system, and the mass of the nation to become more cruelly apparent. There was no revolution whatsoever in agricultural methods; misery increased in the provinces that rebelled or were adjacent to war zones or were subjected to the extensive demands of royal fiscal policy.

Perhaps at a certain date, 1636 or 1637, if agreement had been possible concerning the conditions of a sound peace in foreign affairs, the France that had reestablished her prestige among nations within a few years might have witnessed a very rapid rise in the standard of living of her inhabitants and a more equitable distribution of wealth through her society. The matter is uncertain, for it would be necessary to understand better than we do today the conditions of world economy at that time. But it is beyond a doubt that the prolongation of the war was a catastrophe for everyone. Richelieu knew this well and did not cease to work for the return of peace. We are forced to recognize, however, that this deplorable war brought greater ruin to our adversaries than to us and that it gained for us alone some advantages in Europe. From 1637 to 1642, how great was the increase of public misery and how many abysses were skirted, but also, in this Europe that was so aware of our difficulties and searched for our slightest weakness, what strengthening of our authority, what power, and how many conquests and trophies in our hands!

So many frightful sacrifices were therefore not undertaken in vain.

In *L'Etrange Défaite*, Marc Bloch set down this memorable thought: "There are two categories of Frenchmen who will never understand the history of France, those who refuse to be stirred by the memory of the coronation at Reims and those who read the account of the Festival of Federation without emotion." And he added with profound wisdom, "The present orientation of their preferences matters little."[3] In fact, the greatest error in historical matters is to search the past for attitudes to lift out of context and not to realize that the greatness of certain men and events depends on the quality of their intelligence and their effectiveness *in the conditions of their epoch.* A whole portion of French history finds its place under the symbol of the coronation at Reims, another springs from the act of federation, and between them there was the Revolution. Richelieu became one of the builders of his country's greatness by bringing to the support of a concrete program all the latent strength of a society that was then religious and monarchical.

Many mistakes were made, especially in the liberal and parliamentary nineteenth century—that century which moreover was so respectable and fruitful and toward which our own sometimes shows itself ungrateful—by attributing to Richelieu and the France of his age ideas and sentiments that were completely foreign to them. The presence of the consecrated king was not an annoyance or handicap to Richelieu's work as minister nor even a peril to which he became accustomed; it provided the circumstances that were essential to his acts. Richelieu resorted to many Machiavellian methods, ruses, and pretenses, but no one can deny that he believed with all his might in the superior and religious character of the monarchical principle and the divine mandate in the greatness of his prince. The sovereign himself, who was neither a man of first rank nor a mediocrity and who, two centuries later, would have followed his personal bent and become a junior officer in the wars in Algeria or, if we picture him as a ruling prince in the present political order, a very reasonable constitutional monarch, experienced the same faith in the mission of which he was but the instrument. This faith alone raised him to the eminence of his task. It imparted to him, when necessary, the language that ensured obedience about him.

It is very clear that this obedience was not easily obtained because it required the sacrifice of personal interests that were far from unreasonable or mean. Society as a whole, however, was religious; it closely linked the concept of the king with that of God. Rebels died with the comfort of the sacraments, while

---

[3] M. Bloch, *L'Etrange Défaite*, Paris, 1957, p. 210.

denouncing their rebellion as a sin. Royal authority always clothed itself with divine authority and, when the opposition rose above the individual and sought to make use of principles, it usually invoked religion in order to examine whether royal policy might not have strayed into ways that were prejudicial to the Catholic cause.

This religious conception of the world easily ensured acceptance of hierarchy and privilege, and not because of mere servility or passivity. The Church provided, especially in its organization, the model of a hierarchy and aristocratic society. The doctrine promulgated at Trent bound the Church Militant to the Church Afflicted and the Church Triumphant by a series of intercessions; it led from the saints and the Virgin up to God. The worship of the angels, saints, and the Virgin Mary guided one to the worship of God; all of this was expressed in works of theology as well as the iconography of churches and the imagery of private residences and reinforced the idea that since the temporal order reflected the divine, it was reasonable and just for a well-constructed society not to be egalitarian.

The Protestants who were hostile to the rites and distrustful of the letter of Christianity but attached to its spirit found in the Bible and the example of the chosen people arguments that justified the same opinions. The few individuals and small groups who broke away from all religious beliefs tended to enjoy their nonconformity as a privilege and were not at all inclined to spread ideas of emancipation. One of the freest of these spirits, Cyrano de Bergerac, wrote, "I maintain that popular government is the worst scourge that God may inflict upon a state."[4]. . .

One final characteristic should be recalled. The work of Louis XIII and Richelieu, at once necessary and fearful, masterful and imperfect, remained fragile. For many reasons and primarily because the innovations that it brought did not enter deeply into manners and customs, this intervention of royal authority into so many areas beginning with the fiscal demands of war was accepted only because of the king's power and fear of punishment. What was accomplished did not consist of fundamental reform of the social and economic structure of the nation but

[4] Cited by A. Adam, *Histoire de la littérature française au XVIIe siècle*, Vol. II, *L'Epoque de Pascal*, Paris, 1951, p. 115.

was imposed upon it. Absolutism was above all a practical absolutism that was rendered effective only by the presence of two men. After their disappearance, one is almost amazed to find that in spite of the return to France of the Cardinal's enemies and the adversaries of the policies accepted by Louis XIII, at least a part of their work survived.

The reasons for this—the fidelity of ministers such as Séguier who had served the Cardinal and remained convinced of the efficacy of his undertakings, Mazarin's skill, the acts of financiers who were interested in preserving the system with which they had associated their fortunes, and economic easing during several years—lie outside this study. But it was bound to happen that in the absence of a king old enough to command respect, all groups that had seen their authority decline in the state, the nobility, members of the Parlement, provincial officials, and governing bodies in the cities would seek a return of their earlier favors and prerogatives.

They regrouped very rapidly and, beginning in the summer of 1643, we are able to perceive the first indications of the crisis that would require five years to mature and become the *Fronde*. Specifically, clienteles were formed around such personages as the Abbé de Retz, the future Coadjutor, and the Duke d'Enghien whose youth and victories brought him great prestige. Groups of writers gathered in each other's wake and began to prepare opinion to seek changes.

But great contrasts differentiated the France and Europe of 1643 from those of 1610, and we would never again witness such a degradation of France as had occurred after the death of Henry IV. Gradually, as the years passed by, intimate memory of the miseries of the reign disappeared with their witnesses and victims. And as France rose toward preponderance after the *Fronde* and the strength of the realm seemed to grow in rhythm with that of the young king, the preceding reign came to be viewed favorably. It seemed evident that in all ways the triumphant years of the great century had been prepared by the reign of Louis XIII.

Still later, Cardinal Richelieu was viewed as one of the founders of French unity, one of those who most accurately understood and recognized the character and needs of our nation. An attempt was even made to separate him from the age in which he had lived and, because he had been a precursor, to make him a contemporary. Actually, he was very much a man of his time and this was without doubt his greatest strength because with all his ideals, vigor, and character, he never ceased to appraise judiciously the means at his disposal and to work in the present. There were in him, nevertheless, qualities that do honor to men in all ages and, in the France of Louis XIII, a vigor and youth that enabled him to bear the immense burden of an effort that liberated her from part of her past in order to direct her toward a future of greatness.

6 *Louis Madelin and Ernst H. Kossmann*
The Ruinous and Abortive Fronde

Louis Madelin (1871-1956) and Ernst H. Kossmann who is currently Professor of History at Groningen University in the Netherlands represent very different types of scholarship but have in common the fact that they have published books concerning the Fronde. *The theme of many of Madelin's works is that the French monarchy, even when most absolute, was a legitimate form of government because it mirrored and was grounded upon prevailing conditions and needs in French society. Hence his essentially derogatory treatment of the* Fronde *which he regards as an aberration in the Age of Absolutism. Kossmann's book, which is the best treatment of the* Fronde *available, supports the same general view although in a different manner. Together, these two works clearly show the adverse effects and futility of the* Fronde, *the last massive rebellion against burgeoning absolutism in the seventeenth century.*

SOURCE. The first portion of this selection is from Louis Madelin, *La Fronde*, Paris: Librairie Plon, 1931, pp. 337–341. Translated for this book by William F. Church. Reprinted by permission of Librairie Plon. Copyright 1931 by Librairie Plon. The second portion is from Ernst H. Kossmann, *La Fronde*, Leiden: Universitaire Pers Leiden, 1954, pp. 259–261. Translated for this book by William F. Church. Reprinted by permission of the Universitaire Pers Leiden and the author. Copyright 1954 by the University of Leiden Press.

Although the *Fronde* succeeded in winning only a limited following, it nevertheless sufficed to spread all manner of ruin throughout the land. It was not without consequence that efforts were made in ten provinces to arouse civil war. To nip these initiatives toward sedition in the bud, it was necessary to send in troops, themselves infected with the spirit of indiscipline and therefore dangerous. It was similarly momentous that in six jurisdictions, the Parlements took up political activity and abandoned the dispensing of justice, thereby destroying it. And it was even more consequential that for five years the government of a great country was paralyzed by the mere effort to repress revolt, disorganized by changing its secretaries of state, leaderless when it lost its first minister, divided against itself, and entirely absorbed with the need of preserving its very life. From these circumstances there arose throughout the country an anarchy that was already general after two years and became frightful after five.

I shall pass over the political ruins: the royal family divided, the Parlement's suicide, the assemblies discredited, the momentary loss of all authority by the agents of the crown, but one may say more generally that all the governing classes lost their prestige for a long time to come. National discipline was thoroughly in need of restoration.

Likewise, I shall quickly pass over the moral ruins. The *Fronde* was not a mere political crisis. I have tried to show what a crusade was mounted after Richelieu's death against all discipline. It triumphed momentarily but cruelly in the revolt. The resulting looseness of manners became dreadful and gave rise to a moral debauchery that found its counterpart in strange religious libertinism. Was it not Retz who, although not easily scandalized, nevertheless felt strongly moved when describing how some gentlemen *frondeurs* charged a funeral procession with sword in hand, pointing to the crucifix and shouting, "There is the enemy"? And is this surprising when a series of plays and poems that appeared between 1649 and 1652 parodied hymns and psalms, while sacrilegeous acts in the churches multiplied, such as snatching the host from the hands of the priest so as to "force Jesus Christ to show himself"?

Material ruin spread like a type of plague. Although the crisis was relatively brief, it seemed to condemn the land to lose all the fruits of the slow restoration that had been accomplished since the end of the great civil wars of the sixteenth century. Among other documents, one should read the report of the vicar general, Féret, to the Archbishop of Paris, dated October 25, 1652, to obtain an idea of the condition of the countryside. "Localities, villages and hamlets deserted and without clergy; streets and neighborhoods infected by carrion; the stench of exposed corpses; houses without doors, windows or partitions and many without roofs and reduced to cesspools and stables; all women and girls taking flight; . . . the sick languishing, moribund and dying 'with nothing to comfort them'; peasants living on 'water and grass,' others on 'roots that have lost their strength'; pillaged churches without masses and the dead without graves. There have been no harvests nor vintages, everything having been abandoned to pillage and the ill will of the soldiers so that there is general destitution."

This grievous picture of the beautiful Île-de-France from convincing witnesses permits us to regard it as valid for half the realm. There occurred a curious case of national hemiplegia:[1] with the brain attacked—I mean the royal government held in check by the factions—part of the body was quickly paralyzed. Fields were abandoned; the professions ceased to function; the shops closed. Depopulation was general. In a given city, births during the final three years of the revolt dropped from eighty-six to fifty-two [per thousand], while deaths rose from fifty-eight to two hundred and twenty-four.

"The soldiers," wrote Patin as early as May 24, 1650, "are so ruining the countryside that all the people are even fleeing the cities." These soldiers were those of both throne and rebels. Vincent de Paul wrote, "Wherever men at arms have passed, they have committed sacrilege, thefts and impieties . . . not only in Guyenne and Périgord but in Saintonge, Poitou, Burgundy, Champagne and Picardy." A decree of the royal council in 1658, discharging the inhabitants of all northern France of part of their debts contracted since 1635, testified to the grinding misery into which the latest crisis had thrown France. Was the *Fronde*

---

[1] Paralysis of one-half of the body. (Editor's note.)

responsible for all this? Had not the troopers always acted in this manner? "No," answered Pontis, good soldier that he was, for when he recruited a regiment in 1649, this venerable captain found "a great difference between these troops and those that he had commanded under Louis XIII." This resulted, he added, "from the moral disorder that ordinarily accompanies all civil wars." Goulas, the secretary of Gaston d'Orléans, heard the peasants corroborate Pontis' statement. "Before the uproar in Paris," they said, "everything was going fine. . . . Whenever a peasant complained, he immediately received satisfaction provided he indicated the regiment that was the subject of his complaint. When the investigation was made and the matter verified, the commander made good the damage to the fellow." It would require Le Tellier, as Secretary of State and War, ten years to reestablish discipline and a less deplorable regime.

"Before the uproar in Paris," wrote Goulas. It was from this uproar that the country now dated its misery. And tearful eyes once more turned, as after the misery of the Hundred Years' War and the Wars of Religion, toward the natural restorer, the king, whose acts had too long been paralyzed by the "uproar in Paris."

* * *

I do not deny that my interpretation of the *Fronde* is thoroughly negative. Neither a parliamentary, a popular, nor a feudal revolution seems to have been possible in the France of the seventeenth century, and consequently the *Fronde* remained a period of impetuosity and turbulence without direction or objective. In attempting to be everything at once, it was nothing. It was nothing because the opposition never concentrated its action and thought on a single essential point, attacking with all its strength certain principles and instituions that were generally considered reprehensible.

Certainly, many astonishingly modern and radical ideas were advanced by extremists among the theorists, and they deserve a place in the history of ideas; but it is nevertheless true that, in the whole of the *Fronde* and the actual state of affairs during the period, they remained isolated and gratuitous. They seem to have been an expression of a type of thought which, misguided and quickened by years of anarchy, sought unknown terrain without regard for consequences. They were purely abstract: things that are easy to conceive when one allows oneself to be carried away by a logic that frees itself increasingly from its past. . . . They expressed unrest, but incompletely and without relevance. . . .

The *Fronde* therefore lacked the quality that more than anything else renders a historical phenomenon interesting: it had no creative significance. It seems that in order to be important and compel analysis, a phenomenon must bear upon the future, accelerating or emphasizing the development of certain factors that remain hidden or are slow to evolve. The *Fronde* added nothing to history, neither a new idea susceptible of development nor a new cycle of growth. It doubled back on itself, encased in the limits of its own impotence. It neither anticipated future trends nor revived ancient concepts. It failed to expand and remained locked in its position in time.

It presents, however, an interest of another order. Because it was negative, by analyzing it we may penetrate even into the depths of the French state. The singular structure that was called absolute monarchy opens its doors or, more exactly, the *Fronde* permits the curious spectacle of a vivisection. One after another, the constituant elements of society appear before us. Populace, bourgeoisie, Parliamentarians, and provincials reveal to us the secret nature of their hates and desires. Surely these remained unfulfilled, but we now see what conflicts and tensions were hidden below the surface of the state. And we know more. It seems that the so-called absolute state was peculiar in that it did not coordinate the interests of its subjects but resisted them, and was not a construction that embraced as far as possible all the desires of its inhabitants but placed them in equilibrium. It resulted from neutralization rather than unity and was the sum of discontents and opposing forces in balance. . . .

From the standpoint of this truth, the extreme fragmentation that was revealed by the *Fronde* is entirely normal. The *Fronde* resulted from a ruptured equilibrium or, more exactly, it was identical with the destruction of that equilibrium, the very fact of the rupture. In his desire to analyze the mechanism of this complex state, the historian profits from the impudence with which the *Fronde* lays bare for him the secrets of the majesty of absolutism.

PART THREE

The Reign of Louis XIV

SOURCES

1
Louis XIV
On Kingship

In 1666, Louis XIV conceived the project of committing to paper his knowledge and experience in government for the benefit of the Dauphin. The result was Louis XIV's Memoirs. *The historical value of the work has been disputed because it was compiled by Périgny, preceptor of the Dauphin, and Louis' secretary, Pellisson, was never completed, and contains very little from the pen of the king. How-ever, since Louis authorized the work, was in close touch with its composition, and read and corrected portions of it, we may accept it as accurately reflecting such a fundamental matter as his concept of kingship. In the portions of the* Memoirs *translated here, Louis XIV is shown to have been a firm believer that absolute rule by kings who are "born to possess all and command all" should suffer no human limitation. At the same time, he felt a great sense of obligation to the state because of his enormous responsibilities, and he urged the Dauphin never to shirk his duties as king, however unpleasant they might be. That Louis XIV took seriously the burdens of his "profes-sion of king" is clear both from the* Memoirs *and the record of his reign, yet he also relished the glory and renown that were his as the most powerful monarch in Europe. Service to his state and increasing his personal prestige were but twin aspects of the enormously conse-quential role to which he was destined. Such was Louis XIV's view of royal absolutism in which the king served, controlled, and sym-bolized the state.*

SOURCE. *Mémoires de Louis XIV*, C. Dreyss, ed., Paris, 1860, Vol. II, pp. 370–371, 403–405, 426–432, 230, 518–520. Translated for this book by William F. Church. Published in 1860 by Didier et Cie., Paris.

My son, many very important considerations caused me to resolve to leave you, at the cost of much labor in the midst of my most important duties, these memoirs of my reign and principal acts. I never believed that kings, feeling as they do within themselves great paternal affection and tenderness, might be exempt from the common and natural obligation of fathers to instruct their children by example and advice. On the contrary, it seems to me that in the high rank where you and I find ourselves, public duty is joined to private, and since all the respect that we receive and all the richness and splendor with which we are surrounded are but the rewards that heaven itself associates with the care of the people and states that are confided to us, this care would not be sufficiently great if it did not extend beyond us, causing us to communicate all our knowledge to him who will reign after us.

I even hoped that in this way I might be the most valuable person in the world to you and consequently to my subjects. For no one with more talent and experience has ever reigned in France, and I do not hesitate to say to you that the higher one's position, the more it has qualities that no one may perceive or understand without occupying it. . . .

Although a prince should hold to the maxim that in all things he should initially follow the ways of kindness and that it is more advantageous to persuade his subjects than to coerce them, it is nevertheless true that as soon as he perceives opposition or rebellion, the interests of his glory and even of his subjects require that he enforce strict obedience to himself.

For it is generally agreed that nothing preserves the happiness and tranquillity of the provinces with greater certainty than the perfect union of all authority in the person of the sovereign.

The slightest division of authority always produces the greatest misfortunes, and whether the alienated portion falls into the hands of individuals or groups, it cannot remain there except in a state of violence.

The prince who should restrict authority to himself may not permit it to be divided without making himself responsible for all the disorders that occur and whose number is infinite.

For without counting the revolts and civil wars that the ambition of the great inevitably produces when it is not suppressed, a thousand other evils arise from the mere inattention of the sovereign. Those who are closest to him, being the first to perceive his weakness, are also the first who wish to profit by it. And since they all have followers who will abet their greed, they give them license to imitate their ways. Thus step by step, corruption spreads everywhere and equally affects all groups.

There is no governor who does not arrogate unjust power to himself, no troops that do not live dissolutely, no noble that does not tyrannize over the peasants, no tax collector or agent who does not demonstrate in his area an insolence the more criminal, since he makes use of royal authority when inflicting injustice.

In this general disorder, it seems impossible for the most upright not to be corrupted. For as soon as he goes against the general current and refuses to follow where his own interests naturally lead him, those who should restrain him are themselves first to provide wrong examples!

However, only the public is the victim of all these crimes; it is only from the weak and wretched that so many persons attempt to wrest their monstrous fortunes. Instead of one king that the people should have, they are ruled simultaneously by a thousand tyrants. But there is this difference: the commands of the legitimate prince are always kind and moderate because they are founded on reason, whereas those of these false sovereigns are always unjust and tyrannical because they are inspired by unbridled passion. . . .

As for the work [of governing], my son, . . . I imposed upon myself the rule to labor twice daily. I cannot tell you what benefit I received immediately after making this resolution. I felt elevated in spirit and courage, a changed man, discovering in myself unknown resources and joyfully reproaching myself for having ignored them for so long. . . . I now seemed to be king and born to be so. I finally experienced a joy that is difficult to express and that you yourself will know only when you relish it as I did. . . .

I ordered the four secretaries of state to sign nothing without speaking to me of it. Likewise the superintendent was to do nothing relative to finance without its being entered in a book that was always with me, containing an exact summary where I could see at a glance the state of the treasury at any time and the expenses that were paid or soon would be.

The Chancellor received a similar order, that is, to seal nothing without my command except letters of justice, since it would be unjust to refuse them. . . .

As for those who were to assist me in my work, I resolved above all else not to appoint a first minister. . . . For in order to unite in myself all sovereign authority, I resolved after I had chosen my ministers to call upon them when they least expected it, even though their duties might involve details to which my role and dignity would not ordinarily allow me to stoop, so as to convince them that I would follow the same procedure regarding other matters at any time. The knowledge that resulted from this small step, which I took but rarely and more for diversion than because of any principle, instructed me gradually without effort regarding a thousand things that were of value in making general decisions and which we should understand and carry out in person if it were possible for a single man to know and do all. . . .

Kings who are born to possess all and command all should never be ashamed to seek renown. It is a good that must be constantly and increasingly sought and is more capable than anything else of bringing success to our endeavors. Reputation alone often accomplishes more than the most powerful armies. All conquerors have advanced more with their names than their swords; their mere presence has beaten down a thousand ramparts capable of resisting all their assembled forces. . . .

Kings are often obliged to do things contrary to their inclinations and good nature. They should enjoy giving pleasure, but they must frequently punish and ruin persons whose good they naturally desire. The interest of the state should take precedence. One should counter one's inclinations and not place oneself in position to regret mishandling something important because some individual's interest interfered and diverted attention from the aims that one should have for the grandeur, the good, and the power of the state. Whenever matters give pain, many are delicate and difficult to disentangle. One becomes confused. While this lasts, one may remain indecisive. But as soon as one has taken a position and believes it to be the best choice, it must be carried out. It is this that often caused me to succeed in what

I have done. The mistakes that I have made and have given me infinite pain have been caused by kindness or allowing myself to be too easily guided by others' advice. Nothing is as dangerous as weakness of any kind whatsoever. To command others, one must raise onself over them and, having listened to counsel from all sides, make the decision according to one's best judgment without preoccupation, always seeking to order nothing intrinsically unworthy of the dignity that one bears or the grandeur of the state. Princes who have good intentions and some knowledge of affairs, either through experience or study and great diligence in developing their capabilities, find so many circumstances that cause them to realize that they should give individual care and general attention to everything. One must beware of oneself and one's inclinations, and always be on guard against one's nature. The profession of king is grand, noble, and delightful when one feels capable of acquitting himself well in everything that he undertakes. But he is not exempt from pain, fatigue, and anxiety. Uncertainty sometimes drives one to despair, but when one has spent a reasonable time examining a matter, one must decide and choose the course that one thinks best. When the state is one's concern, one works for oneself. The good of the one gives rise to the glory of the other. When the state is happy, eminent, and powerful, he who has brought this about derives glory from it and consequently, as between himself and his subjects, should enjoy more than they all that is agreeable in life.

2   *Jacques-Bénigne Bossuet*
The Majesty and Justice of Kings

Jacques-Bénigne Bossuet (1627–1704), Bishop of Meaux, is famous as court preacher and leader of the French clergy during the reign of Louis XIV. He is also known as one of the major proponents of

SOURCE. Jacques-Bénigne Bossuet, *Oeuvres oratoires*, C. Urbain et E. Levesque, eds., Paris: Librairie Hachette, 1921, Vol. IV, pp. 360–364, 373, 375–376. Translated for this book by William F. Church. Reprinted by permission of Librairie Hachette. Copyright 1921 by Librairie Hachette, Paris.

the theory of divine right of kings. Because of his great influence at the royal court and the favor with which Louis XIV regarded him, Bossuet's political ideas may be said to have enjoyed semiofficial standing. The present selection is taken from his "Sermon on the Duties of Kings," which he delivered before Louis XIV on April 2, 1662. Here Bossuet attributes divinity to both kingship and individual kings, thus pushing the divine right of kings to its furthest limit. He insisted, however, that there were limits on royal power and discretion: those of Christian justice. Such was his simple but exalted view of monarchy in which the king was responsible to God and should rule in accordance with Christian morality, but without limitation by any human agency. Because this sermon was actually delivered before the king, the political ideas that it contains may have been more widely accepted at the royal court than the more complex interpretation of kingship in Bossuet's better-known Politique tirée des propres paroles de l'Ecriture sainte, *which remained unpublished until after his death.*

"By me kings reign,"[1] says eternal Wisdom, and from this we should conclude not only that the rights of royalty are established by his laws but the choice of rulers is an effect of his providence. . . . "There is no power but of God," [2] says the oracle of the Scriptures. . . .

In order to establish this power, which represents his own, God places on the foreheads of sovereigns and on their visages a mark of divinity. . . . "You are gods," said David; "you are all sons of the Most High."[3] But O gods of flesh and blood, O gods of earth and dust, "you will die like men."[4] No matter, you are gods. Although you will die, your authority will not; the spirit of royalty passes intact to your successors and everywhere inspires the same respect and veneration. The man dies, it is true, but the king, as we say, never dies. The image of God is immortal.

It is therefore easy to understand that of all living persons, none

[1] Proverbs VIII, 15.
[2] Romans XIII, 1.
[3] Psalm LXXXII, 6.
[4] Psalm LXXXII, 7.

should be more conscious of God's majesty than kings, for how may they forget Him whose active, distinct and ever-present image they always carry within themselves? The prince feels in his heart the vigor, strength, and noble confidence to command; he knows that he has only to move his lips and at once all is set in motion from one end of the realm to the other. . . . And when he penetrates the most secret plots, with his long reach he overtakes his enemies in the far corners of the earth and deters them, so to speak, from plunging into the abyss where they seek refuge. How easy it is to imagine the controls and watchfulness of God as irresistible! But when the king sees the people in subjection, obliged to obey him "not only because of wrath but also for conscience' sake,"[5] as the Apostle says, how can he ever forget that he owes all to the living and eternal God to whom all hearts speak and from whom no consciences hold secrets? . . .

So many forceful considerations should induce kings to be continually conscious of the Gospel, always to heed this higher law, to allow themselves nothing that God does not permit, and never to let their power stray beyond the bounds of Christian justice. Surely they would provide God with too apt a reason for reproval if, among the many benefits that He gives them, they were to seek others in pleasures that He forbids, use against him the power that He gives them, and violate the laws that they were established to protect.

Here is the peril of the great of the earth. Like other men, they must combat their passions; more than all others they must check their own power. For, as it is absolutely necessary for men to be restrained by something, the powers under which all bend should themselves recognize their limits. It is in this, said Gregory the Great, that lies the noblest wisdom of royalty, . . . the most necessary truth for a Christian king to comprehend: "Only he who knows how to restrict power understands how to use it. . . ."

Christians! Justice is the true virtue of monarchs and the sole support of majesty. For what is majesty? It is not a certain commanding presence on the prince's countenance and his whole exterior; it is a more penetrating splendor that creates deferential

[5] Romans XIII, 5.

fear in all hearts. This splendor arises from justice; we have a
fine example in the story of King Solomon. . . . "All Israel," say
the Scriptures, "learned that the king had judged, and they
feared the king, knowing that the wisdom of God was in him."[6]
His exalted mien caused him to be loved, but his justice caused
him to be feared with that respectful fear that does not destroy
love but renders it more serious and circumspect. It is this love
mingled with fear that is born of justice, and with it the true
character of majesty. . . .

Sire, you know the needs of your people, the burdens beyond
their strength with which they are saddled. Something great
and magnificent beyond the destiny of earlier kings, your predecessors, is stirring for you. Be faithful to God and do not cause
your sins to place any obstacle in the path of those things that
impend. Carry the glory of your name and that of France to
such heights that there may be nothing for you to desire but
eternal felicity.

3   *Jean Domat*
               The Ideal Absolute State

*Jean Domat (1625–1696) was one of the ablest French jurists dur-
ing the reign of Louis XIV. In the course of a distinguished legal
career, he made it his objective to recast the chaotic body of French
law (medieval customs, royal ordinances, and Roman legal precepts)
according to the principles of natural law and Christian morality.
Since his project coincided with Louis XIV's desire to give France
a single code of laws, Domat was given an annual pension by the
king and completed his work under royal sponsorship. His books
were published by the royal printer, and their contents may be said
to have enjoyed semiofficial status. Although Domat's treatises were*

[6] III Kings, III, 28.

SOURCE: Jean Domat, *Le Droit public*, Paris, 1697, Book I, Preliminary
Section and Titles I, II. Translated for this book by William F. Church.

never incorporated into the legislative reforms of the reign, they were hailed as major contributions to legal science and caused him to be esteemed as the ablest legal philosopher of the age. The selection that is given here is from his treatment of French public law and may be regarded as an officially approved analysis of the ideal absolute state as it was understood by those in the seats of power.

There is no one who is not convinced of the importance of good order in the state and who does not genuinely desire to see well regulated the state in which he is obliged to spend his life. For everyone knows . . . that this order concerns and affects him in many ways. . . .

All know that human society forms a body of which each person is a member. This truth, which Scripture teaches us and the light of reason makes evident, is the foundation of all the duties that determine each man's conduct toward all others and toward the whole. For these duties are nothing but the functions that are proper to the position in which each man finds himself according to his rank in the body.

It is in this principle that one must seek the source of all the precepts and duties of those who govern and of those who are their subjects. For it is by placing each person in the body of society that God . . . prescribes his functions and duties by thus calling him. And as He commands all scrupulously to observe the precepts of his law that bind all in common, He also prescribes each man's individual duties that are determined by his condition and the status that he occupies in the body of which he is a member. . . .

All men being equal by nature because of the humanity that is their essence, nature does not cause some to be inferior to others. But in this natural equality, they are separated by other principles that render their conditions unequal and give rise to relationships and dependencies that determine their varying duties toward others and render government necessary. . . .

The first distinction that subjects some persons to others is that which birth introduces between parents and children. . . . The second distinction among persons is that which requires different employments in society and unites all in the body of which each is a member. For, since God caused each man to require the services of several others to satisfy his wants, He differentiated among their conditions and pursuits in order to meet all their needs, giving all their places in which they should fulfill their functions. And it is these varying occupations and dependencies that create the ties that form society among men, as those of its members form a body. This renders it necessary that a head coerce and rule the body of society and maintain order among those who should give the public the benefit of the different contributions that their stations require of them. . . .

This necessity of government over men whom nature created equal but who differ among themselves according to the diversity that God established in their conditions and professions demonstrates that government results from His ordering. As He is the only natural sovereign over men, it is from Him that all who govern hold their power and authority, and it is God himself that they represent in their functions. . . .

Since government is necessary for the common good and God himself established it, it follows that those who are its subjects must be submissive and obedient. For otherwise they would resist God, and the government which should be the source of the peace and unity that make possible the public good would suffer from dissention and trouble that would destroy it. . . .

As obedience is necessary to preserve the order and peace that unite the head and members of the body of the state, it is the universal obligation of all subjects in all cases to obey the ruler's orders without assuming the liberty of judging them. For otherwise each man would be master because of his right to examine what might be just or unjust, and this liberty would favor sedition. Thus every man owes obedience even to unjust laws and orders, provided that he may execute and obey them without injustice. And the only exception that may exempt him from this obligation is limited to cases in which he may not obey without violating divine law.

The power of the sovereign government should be in proportion to its ministry and its rank in the human society that constitutes the state, since he who is its head fills the place of God. For as God is the sole natural ruler of men, their judge, legislator, and king, there can be no legitimate authority of one man over all others unless he holds it from the hand of God. Thus the power of sovereigns is a participation in that of God; it is like the arm and the strength of the justice that should be the spirit of government and alone has natural authority over the minds and hearts of men. . . .

According to these principles, which are the natural foundations of the authority of those who govern, their power should have two essential attributes: first, to cause justice to rule without exception and, second, to be as absolute as the rule of justice, that is, as absolute as the rule of God Himself who is justice, rules according to its principles, and desires rulers to do likewise. . . .

Since the power of princes comes to them from God and is placed in their hands as an instrument of his providence and his guidance of the states that He commits to their rule, it is clear that princes should use their power in proportion to the objectives that providence and divine guidance seek . . . and that power is confided to them to this end. This is without doubt the foundation and first principle of all the duties of sovereigns that consist of causing God Himself to rule, that is, regulating all things according to His will, which is nothing more than justice. The rule of justice should be the glory of the rule of princes. . . .

The power of sovereigns includes the authority to exercise the functions of government and to use the force that is necessary to their ministry. For authority without force would be despised and almost useless, while force without legitimate authority would be mere tyranny. . . .

There are two uses of sovereign power that are necessary to the public tranquillity. One consists of constraining the subjects to obey and repressing violence and injustice, the other of defending the state against the aggressions of its enemies. Power should be accompanied by the force that is required for these two functions.

The use of force for the maintenance of public tranquillity within the state includes all that is required to protect the sovereign himself from rebellions that would be frequent if authority and force were not united, and all that is required to keep order among the subjects, repress violence against individuals and the general public, execute the orders of the sovereign, and effect all that is required for the administration of justice. Since the use of force and the occasions that require it are never-ending, the government of the sovereign must maintain the force that is needed for the rule of justice. This requires officials and ministers in various functions and the use of arms whenever necessary. . . .

One should include among the rights that the law gives the sovereign that of acquiring all the evidences of grandeur and majesty that are needed to bring renown to the authority and dignity of such great power and to instill awe in the minds of the subjects. For although the latter should view royal power as from God and submit to it regardless of tangible indications of grandeur, God accompanies his own power with a visible majesty that extends over land and sea. . . . When He wishes to exercise his august power as lawgiver, He proclaims his laws with prodigies that inspire reverence and unspeakable terror. He is therefore willing that sovereigns enhance the dignity of their power . . . in such manner as to win the respect of the people. . . .

The general duties . . . of those who have sovereign authority include all that concern the administration of justice, the general polity of the state, public order, tranquillity of the subjects, security of families, attention to all that may contribute to the general good, the choice of skillful ministers who love justice and truth, . . . discrimination between justice and clemency whenever justice might suffer from relaxation of its rigor, wise distribution of benefits, rewards, exemptions, privileges and other concessions, wise administration of the public funds, prudence regarding foreigners, and all that may render government agreeable to the good, terrible to the wicked, and entirely worthy of the divine function of ruling men by wielding power that comes only from God and is a participation in his own.

As the final duty of the sovereign, one may add the following which stems from the administration of justice and includes all others. Although his power seems to place him above the law, since no man has the right to call him to account for his conduct, he should observe the laws that concern himself not only because he should be an example to his subjects and render their duty pleasant but because he is not dispensed from his own duty by his sovereign power. On the contrary, his rank obliges him to subordinate his personal interests to the general good of the state, which it is his glory to regard as his own.

4   *Jean-Baptiste Colbert*
The Regulation of Commerce and Industry

Jean-Baptiste Colbert (1619–1683) is well known as one of history's most energetic practitioners of mercantilism. Although Louis XIV saddled him with many other responsibilities, Colbert always devoted his primary attention to regulating the French economy according to the fashionable doctrines of bullionism and protectionism. The matrix of economic precepts and practices that is usually called "mercantilism" may be regarded as the economics of state building during the Age of Absolutism, and Colbert was thoroughly convinced that by applying maximum controls he could extensively strengthen the economy of the state. Because Colbert was an administrator and man of action rather than a writer, he left few analyses of his work. The present selection is from his report to the king in the Council of Commerce, August 3, 1664, and is one of the best statements of his program to come from his pen. The reader will note that his entire emphasis is upon regulating French commerce and industry so as to increase the wealth of the state, that is, the money available to it. In the process, the subjects might be benefited, but Colbert's primary purpose was to strengthen the state and increase royal power.

Sire, since it pleases your majesty to give a few hours of your attention to the reestablishment or rather the establishment of the commerce of your realm, although this is something that concerns only the good of your subjects and gives your majesty no advantage except hope for the future after increasing the

SOURCE. *Lettres, Instructions et Mémoires de Colbert*, P. Clement, ed., Paris, 1863, Vol. II, pp. cclxiii, cclxvii–cclxxii. Translated for this book by William F. Church. Published in 1863 by the Librairie Imperiale, Paris.

wealth of your people, and even though frequent discussion of commerce annoys your majesty because it is rather disagreeable in itself and involves diminution of your revenue, it is certain, Sire, that when your majesty sacrifices two things that are so important and dear to a king, first, the time that you might devote to amusements and other more agreeable matters and, second, your revenue, by this unparalleled evidence of your love of your people, you will endlessly multiply their veneration and respect for you and the admiration of foreigners. . . .

Undertakings that are easy produce little or no glory and advantage; only the difficult do so. If, to the natural power of France, the king is able to add that which the art and business of commerce is capable of producing, cursory reflection on the power of the cities and states that merely share in this art and business will easily indicate that the king's grandeur and power will be prodigiously increased. . . .

As for ruining the Dutch, such things are never total. France does not have at present two hundred seaworthy ships in her ports; in 1658 the Dutch had sixteen thousand. It is merely a question of the massive diligence and protection of the king augmenting his subjects' vessels in eight or ten years, perhaps to as many as two thousand. Of this figure, the Dutch will probably lose twelve or fifteen hundred, and other nations the difference. Thus it is not a question of ruining them but merely a small diminution of their vessels.

The king's power on land is superior to that of all the nations of Europe, but on the sea it is inferior. This is the only means of making it equal everywhere.

The Dutch well know that their commerce and their state will gain much in alliance with France but will lose everything with others. The difficulties that the Dutch East India Company will experience in purchasing goods in the Indies and selling them in Europe cannot be overcome without the power and protection of the king and even his financial aid whenever necessary. The final reason [for this policy] is that in observing your treaties with the Dutch, your majesty is obliged to prefer the good of your subjects to that of your allies.

After discussing the reasons for the king's endeavoring to reestablish commerce, it is fitting to examine in detail the state to which it was reduced when your majesty began to assume the direction of affairs.

For commerce within the realm and between ports:

Factories for manufacturing broadcloth, serge and other stuffs of high quality, papers, hardware, silks, linens, soap, and generally all other means of production were and still are almost entirely ruined.

The Dutch have hindered [our manufacturing] all of these products and bring them to us in order to take from us in exchange the commodities that are necessary for their consumption and trade. On the other hand, if factories to produce these goods were reestablished, not only would we have them for our own use, so that the Dutch would be obliged to give us the money they now keep, we would even have commodities to send abroad to bring us a comparable return in money, which is, in a word, the sole aim of commerce and the only means of increasing the grandeur and power of this state.

As for seagoing commerce, either between ports or with foreign lands, since there are only two to three hundred vessels belonging to the king's subjects in all the ports of the realm, it is certain that the Dutch take annually from the realm, according to exact calculation, four million *livres* for transportation costs, for which they carry off our products. Since these products are absolutely necessary to them, if we had sufficient vessels for this transportation from port to port, they would be obliged to bring us the same amount in ready cash.

The reasons for the poor condition of internal commerce are:

The debts of cities and communities, which prevent communication—the principle of all the commerce of the king's subjects from province to province and city to city.

The legal wrangles that these debts have produced in the cities, impoverishing the inhabitants.

The number of tolls everywhere on land and water.

The ruin of public roads.

The horrible multiplicity of officials.

Excessive taxes on all commodities.

Excessive and badly handled tolls at the borders of provinces and the realm.

Piracy, which has caused the loss of a great many vessels.

And, in a word, the inattention of the king and his council, causing the same among all lesser officials who have regulatory authority in their hands for protecting and increasing all manufactures.

For foreign commerce:

It is certain that, with the exception of some vessels from Marseilles that go to the Levant, there is no such commerce in the realm. Even the trade with the American islands that are inhabited by the French is entirely handled by one hundred and fifty Dutch vessels, which send them foodstuffs from Germany and manufactured goods from Holland, returning sugar, tobacco, and chemicals for dyes to the homeland. There the Dutch levy import duties on these commodities, change them into finished products, pay export duties on them, and bring them to us. Merchandise of this type amounts annually to two million *livres,* for which they take away the same quantity of our needed products. If we ourselves carried on this trade with our islands, the Dutch would be obliged to bring us the two million in ready cash.

Having succinctly shown the condition of domestic and foreign trade, it would perhaps not be inappropriate to indicate briefly the advantages of commerce.

I believe that all readily accept the principle that only an abundance of money in a state may increase its grandeur and power.

From this standpoint, it is certain that basic commodities to the value of twelve to eighteen million *livres* annually leave the realm to be consumed abroad. (These commodities are wines, brandies, vinegar, iron, fruits, papers, linens, hardware, silks, and cottons.) These are the mines of our realm whose conservation must be diligently sought.

The Dutch and other foreigners wage perpetual war against these mines and until now have been so successful that instead of this sum entering the realm in ready money and producing great abundance, they bring in various commodities, manufactured by themselves or other foreigners, valued at two-thirds of this sum. . . .

Their industry and our lack of intelligence have advanced so far that, by means of their agents and commissioners whom they have been able to establish in all the ports of the realm to control all foreign trade, they set the prices of all the merchandise that they buy and sell.

From this, it is easy to conclude that the more we limit the gains of the Dutch from the king's subjects and our consumption of imported goods, the more we shall increase the money that should enter the realm as payment for our primary products. By this amount we shall increase the power, grandeur, and riches of the state.

We may draw the same inference in regard to articles of carrying trade, that is, those that we might transport from the East and West Indies to the northern countries from which we ourselves might bring back the materials needed for building ships, the other portion of the grandeur and power of the state.

In addition to the advantages that the entry of a greater quantity of ready money would produce in the realm, it is certain that these industries would enable a million persons who languish in idleness to earn their living. A considerable number would also support themselves on the sea and in the principle ports, and almost endless multiplication of vessels would proportionally increase the grandeur and power of the state.

These, to my mind, are the objectives toward which the king's efforts, goodness, and love of his people should be directed.

The means of achieving these are:

By a decree of the council, made in your majesty's presence, inform the entire populace, by circulatory letters, of the decision that your majesty has taken.

All who have the honor of serving your majesty should publicize the advantages that this will bring the king's subjects.

Receive all merchants who appear at court with special evidences of protection and good will.

Aid them in all things concerning their commerce, occasionally hearing them in your majesty's council when they come with important matters.

Invite them to appoint some of their members who will always be in the king's retinue.

Order the Grand Marshal of Lodgings always to reserve proper housing for them.

In the absence of deputies, appoint someone with power to correspond with them, receive their dispatches and complaints, petition for them and inform them of all that may be decided for their benefit and advantage.

Renew all local regulations within the realm for the reestablishment of all manufacturing facilities.

Examine all import and export duties; lessen them on products made and to be made, and lighten the burden on manufacturers by 1,200,000 to 1,500,000 *livres* annually.

Devote annually a considerable sum to reestablishing factories and increasing commerce, according to decisions to be made in the council.

The same for navigation, subsidizing all who will buy or build new vessels or undertake long voyages.

Repair the public roads and continue to remove tolls from rivers.

Undertake anew the work of discharging the debts of local communities.

Constantly work to render navigable the rivers of the realm.

Carefully examine communication between the seas through Guyenne and Burgundy.

Strongly support the East and West India Companies.

Urge everyone to participate in them.

Discuss in the king's presence every matter in which merchants are interested.

Send a general dispatch to all trading establishments of the realm, through their presidents and the procurors-general, to inform them of your majesty's decision to take particular care of all that concerns them.

The same to all governors of provinces and cities, all mayors, and sheriffs to inform them also, with orders to assemble the merchants and read it to them in their presence.

Beyond this, each council must examine a specific branch of commerce in detail in order to apply appropriate remedies. For example:

The commerce with the Levant and the disorders caused by the consuls.

All that concerns the East and West India Companies.

Commerce with the north, Archangel, Moscow and the Baltic Sea, Norway.

Tolls within the realm.

Repayment of communities' debts.

Public roads.

Navigation on streams and rivers.

Factories.

Examine seaports and their problems.

5   *Nicolas-Joseph Foucault*
        The Persecution of the Huguenots

Nicolas-Joseph Foucault (1643–1721) is rated as one of Louis XIV's ablest intendants. An efficient administrator, he promoted a variety of public works and sought to improve economic conditions in his several intendancies. His Memoirs, *however, are chiefly notable for his vivid account of the various measures that he took against the Huguenots during Louis XIV's campaign to extirpate Calvinism and restore religious uniformity. Foucault was one of the more aggressive administrators in applying the many anti-Huguenot decrees both before and after the revocation of the Edict of Nantes. The portions of his* Memoirs *that are given here describe his actions in his intendancies of Béarn and Poitou at the height of the persecution. He frankly and sometimes naïvely recounts his use of money and force as well as subtler means in his campaign for conversions, and he clearly indicates the trouble that the royal government experienced in keeping the newly converted from returning to the ways of Calvinism. In these pages, Foucault gives a memorable picture of the human impact of Louis XIV's decision to end religious division within his realm.*

SOURCE: Nicolas-Joseph Foucault, *Mémoires*, F. Baudry, ed., Paris, 1862, pp. 115, 117–121, 125–128, 152–157, 159, 161, 171–172, 174–178, 180–181. Translated for this book by William F. Church. Published in 1862 by the Librairie Imperiale, Paris.

On February 22nd, 1685, I arrived in Pau where all groups vied with each other to show their joy at my return. . . . Two days later I took the edicts and declarations regarding religious matters to the Parlement for their consideration. After these acts had been registered and published, I lost no time in informing the consistories of the proscribed temples concerning the decree that ordered their demolition within one month. This was duly carried out without resistance although the members were very disheartened, as I informed the Chancellor in my letter of March 5th.

After the demolition of fifteen temples, I ordered the Procuror General to charge the remaining five with contravening the edicts and decrees of the council. The lawsuits were quickly completed, and the decrees requiring demolition were executed without delay, so that in less that six weeks there was not a single temple remaining in all Béarn. The demolitions caused the ministers to leave the province and by their desertion these false pastors left me a free field for conversions. . . .

On April 5th, I informed the Chancellor that one of the principal reasons why the Protestants opposed the Catholic missionaries was that the king still permitted the profession of the pretended reformed religion in his realm, . . . but that eleven hundred persons had converted counting children and that there were many noblemen who were wavering and would be brought over by pensions. . . .

On April 18th I asked M. de Louvois for blank orders authorizing the quartering of one or more companies of soldiers in cities that were strongly Protestant, being certain that the mere appearance of the troops would produce a great many conversions. I agreed to maintain such good control that the troops would wreak no violence, and I would hold myself answerable for all complaints that he might receive. . . . M. de Louvois having sent me several blank orders, six hundred persons converted in five cities or boroughs at the mere news that the companies were on the march. . . .

I caused Lord Goulard, a minister of Oloron, to abjure Calvinism in the cathedral of that city in the presence of the bishop and more than eight thousand persons of both religions. He gave such a good account of his reasons for converting that many

Protestants, stirred by the truths that the ministers always hid and were now carefully and faithfully set forth, converted with him. The great majority of the others promised me to seek instruction after being informed that the king's intention was not that they embrace the Roman faith without understanding it but that they should freely examine its dogma and principles. . . .

The Protestants of Orthez sent a courier to the king to learn whether he intended absolutely to forbid the exercise of the pretended reformed religion in Béarn. I asked M. de Croissy not to send Calvinist ministers to baptize children born in the pretended reformed religion and to return the Bishops of Lescar, Oloron, and Dax to their dioceses with missionaries to instruct the newly converted. An extraordinary mission to travel throughout all Béarn is most urgently needed, and the best preachers are none too skillful to take the place of the Calvinist ministers who preach well. All the priests of Béarn are ignorant and often follow evil ways; vicars should be established for them. I proposed that the courier from Orthez be sent to the Bastille.

Of the four thousand Protestants in Orthez three thousand eight hundred converted, which caused me to inform the ministers [at Versailles] that they could assure the king of the total conversion of Béarn. Of twenty-two thousand there remained less than a thousand and nobles were beginning to come over. . . .

From my return to Pau in February until August, fifteen thousand souls converted. There were many who abjured at the approach of the soldiers without seeing them. Distribution of money also won over many to the Church. The Béarnais have an inconstant disposition, and they returned to the religion of their fathers as easily as they were subverted by the Queen, Jeanne d'Albret.

The city of Orthez was the last to be converted, and I sent in soldiers who subdued it. The inhabitants asked for fifteen days in which to be instructed, but this was merely to await the return of the courier who had been sent to the court to request the liberty to practice their religion. At the end of that time they requested eight more days so as to give the courier time to arrive. I refused them and of the four thousand Protestants in Orthez two thousand converted before the troops arrived, so that when I made a circuit there with missionaries, all converted except twenty obstinate families who were resolved not to change, come what might. They were led by a nobleman named Bresselaye who also went to the court and was placed in the Bastille.

Of the twenty-two thousand Protestants in Béarn twenty-one thousand had converted by the end of July.

On August 3rd I informed the Chancellor that eight days earlier the Parlement had issued a decree against Jean Pedelabat, from Garlin, convicting him of publicly and privately urging the Protestants to remain firm in their religion for which he was fined six hundred *livres* and banished from the realm for twenty years. Six days after the decree was issued, he caused me to be notified that he wished to convert, which he did yesterday with all of his family. His conversion with that of his wife and several children justified all that I had asked of the Chancellor....

On August 16th M. de Croissy sent me blank orders to confine obstinate noblemen. On the previous day I had assembled some of the Protestant nobility to inform them of the king's intentions. A dozen nobles converted; the others asked for fifteen days in which to be instructed. I renewed my recommendations to M. de Croissy against giving ministers permission to leave the realm and sell their goods. . . .

On August 18th I informed the Archbishop of Paris that it was most necessary to give pensions to converted ministers and to prevent the unconverted leaving the realm. . . .

On August 27th ninety-seven women converted in the little city of Salies. I also converted many men in the presence of the Marquis de Boufflers. . . .

In August of that year, I was appointed Intendant of Poitou . . . and arrived in Poitiers on September 7th. On the day before my departure from Pau a great many nobles came and converted in my presence. . . . The Lord of Sault, a nobleman of Béarn of the pretended reformed religion, was put in the Bastille for wicked discourse at my request. There had been twenty-two thousand conversions in Béarn....

[On October 17th, 1685, the Edict of Fontainebleau revoked the Edict of Nantes, thereby outlawing Protestantism in France.]

During January, 1686, all the Protestants of Poitiers and Châtellerault converted, and there remained in the province only five or six hundred Protestants, either prisoners or fugitives. . . .

The Lord of Saint-Philbert, a very wealthy nobleman, converted as did the Lady of la Lourrie which produced a large
number of conversions. Imprisonment in a remote area brought
more nobles into the Church than the dragoons. It was prison
that converted the Lord of Gagemont. . . .

I notified M. de Louvois that a major obstacle to conversion
in several parishes was the scandalous life of the priests whom
the bishop could not compel to do their duties by ordinary means
because of appeals from his orders. I sent him the names of
three of these priests who should be sent to the seminary at
Richelieu, which is very well regulated. This was the only means
of disciplining them. The order was issued. . . .

On February 8th I received an order from the king to conduct the Lords of Vesançay, Mauroy, and Gagemont, noblemen
of the pretended reformed religion of Poitou, to the castle of
Pierre-Encise because of their refusal to convert. . . .

On March 3rd I received a letter from M. de Seignelay by
which he informed me of the king's intention to prevent both
the Protestants and the newly converted Catholics leaving the
realm. For this purpose it was necessary to place reliable persons
along the coast of Poitou to prevent their departure; the king
would assume this expense. I sent him a list of the remaining
Protestants in Poitou.

On March 4th M. de Louvois informed me of the king's intention to expand the churches of Poitou which could not
accommodate all who should attend divine service because of the
large number of newly converted. For this his majesty desired
that I have plans, specifications, and contracts drawn up as soon
as possible and that I send him an estimate of what it would cost
to alter the churches according to these plans during the present
year. All this in cooperation with the bishops and with expenses
so regulated that they would involve his majesty only so far as
absolutely necessary to provide cover for the inhabitants of
each parish. . . .

On March 10th M. de Louvois wrote me that the king did not
wish fines to be used to force the newly converted to attend mass. Instead they should have soldiers quartered in their
homes. . . .

During May I pronounced judgment in the court at Poitiers against six Protestants who had been arrested on the Ile de Ré for attempting to flee abroad. I condemned two noblemen and a lawyer to the galleys in perpetuity and three women to perpetual banishment which is not a hardship for fugitives. I also proposed that the king cause the three women to be placed in convents. . . .

The newly converted experienced difficulty in approaching the sacraments, but less in listening to sermons. I proposed to M. de Louvois to send preachers who are good controversialists to be distributed among the cantons where there are many converted, especially in places where there had been temples, and who would preach on Sundays after the manner of the ministers, that is, explaining the Gospel and offering prayers at the end of their sermons as is done in many places. By this means the converted would become accustomed to the mysteries of our religion. . . .

On December 8th an instruction was sent to all commanders and intendants in all provinces where there were Protestants, by which the king prescribed the conduct that should be followed regarding the Protestants in the execution of his majesty's edicts, declarations, decrees of the council, and orders. This instruction especially recommended moderation in the punishments that officials were obliged to impose and was very good in itself, but it could not remain secret and had the quality of a most detrimental relaxation in religious affairs at a time when the hearts of the newly converted were not sufficiently confirmed in the communion of the Roman Church and would inevitably be influenced to return to their earlier beliefs, persuaded by their ministers and the relapsed heretics whom the king does not see fit to compel to attend church. . . .

In 1686 I received an order to levy the *taille* from Protestant nobles, which produced many conversions. Throughout the entire year there were specific orders to watch the coast of Poitou to prevent the Protestants leaving the realm. . . .

The Lord of la Chauvinière, a nobleman of lower Poitou, seemed the most obstinate and voluntarily entered prison at Niort. His son converted and the father was sent to Pierre-Encise.

The women and girls of the pretended reformed religion feared the convents more than the dragoons, and many whom the latter had not been able to convert were now converted because they could not overcome their aversion for the convents. . . .

The Lord of La Primaudaye who seemed to lead the party converted. I had sought means of bringing him into the Church and, because of the respect that I accorded him, he converted and brought many noblemen and others into the Church. Madame de la Forest, sister of M. Dangeau, was among these and her example caused the conversion of many women. . . .

On January 11, 1687, M. de Louvois sent me orders to send six Protestants who were prisoners at Poitiers to Pierre-Encise and five to the citadel at Besançon. Of the women, half were to go to convents in the diocese of Beauvais and half to those in Amiens.

After I notified M. de Louvois that an assembly of newly converted had been held near Pouzauges, he wrote me on January 24th that if this were true I should promptly inflict so severe a punishment upon those who had assembled that the example would give pause to others.

On January 25th he wrote me another letter to initiate proceedings against those who had assembled and to raze the chateaux and houses where the assemblies had taken place. . . .

The Protestants who had assembled near Pouzauges and were made prisoner asked for mercy and promised to live as good Catholics but this was to save their lives. Almost all were wool carders. It was among persons of this trade that Calvinism began in France.

Because the Catholics of long standing in the boroughs of Pouzauges and Moncoutant made no move to prevent the assemblies of the newly converted, did not report them, and did not wish to give evidence of these assemblies, I proposed to the king to send in a company of cavalry.

M. de Louvois wrote me on February 9th that the king's intention was to overwhelm with troops those areas where the inhabitants attended assemblies and sent me a decree to bring action against them.

Another letter of February 14th urged disregarding the evidences of repentance given by four newly converted who were arrested for attending assemblies near Pouzauges and indicated the king's desire to proceed against them. . . .

After a long interval, I finally received a decree of the council appointing me, with the officers of the court at Fontenay, to judge the newly converted who had assembled near Pouzauges. Of the four accused prisoners, one named Bigot who served as minister in these assemblies was condemned to be hanged, two were sent to the galleys, and the fourth was banished in perpetuity, all according to their degree of guilt. During the trial, Bigot seemed to repent, especially while under interrogation; however, he reasserted his errors when he heard his judgment pronounced. He made no public profession of the religion in which he died and merely sang a Psalm, but as he had a weak voice the singing of the *Salve* by the people drowned his voice and no one heard him. He accused no nobleman, minister, nor other person of quality. Although I notified M. de Louvois by letter on February 22nd, the day of sentencing, that I thought it a sufficient example to condemn the preacher to death, since the others might merely have allowed themselves to be attracted to the assemblies, he found that I had been too indulgent and should condemn the four that I had judged. I did not believe that it was by order of the king that he accused me of too much leniency and was convinced that he drew this reproach from his own heart. . . .

On March 11th I received a letter [from M. de Louvois] to send several Protestants who had hidden and been arrested to Pierre-Encise and the women to convents in the dioceses of Meaux and Noyon. . . . On April 10th I sent fifteen Huguenot women to Paris to be placed in convents. . . . On April 16th I sent sixteen Protestant women and girls to Noyon. . . .

The missionaries worked very successfully for conversions.

During June the widow of a minister of Châtellerault hid in the house of one of her neighbors so as to avoid being sought out for her religion. When the officers of Châtellerault received word of this and went to the house, she heard the noise and threw herself into a well from which she was taken and conducted to the female penitentiary of Poitiers. . . .

On August 14, 1687, I informed M. de Louvois that I had

executed with the utmost fidelity the instructions that he had given me, but I feared that they would permit the newly converted great laxity in practicing their religion, of which I already perceived the beginnings.

6   The Condition of the Realm at Mid-Reign (1687)

In 1687, Louis XIV commissioned two very able administrators (Henri Daguesseau, councillor of state, and Antoine d'Ormesson, Master of Requests) to investigate the collection of certain royal taxes in the Orléanais and Le Maine in central France. After they submitted their report, they returned to Paris and had a special audience with the king in order to inform him of the true condition of these provinces. Louis listened to them for a full evening (a major concession), after which he asked them to give him their ideas in writing. Their second report therefore constitutes a vital source concerning conditions in the French countryside at mid-reign. Parts of it are given in this selection. The commissioners frankly describe the extreme poverty that they found and do not hesitate to point to its major cause—excessive royal taxation. They even go so far as to observe that while these levies may have been necessary for the good of the state when they were made, they have had dire effects and threaten the decline of the realm. Their suggested remedies include the restoration of commerce and consumption, but this they viewed as impossible without the diminution of taxation. In other words, they clearly identified the source of rural poverty and left the decision regarding amelioration to the king. Such a frank appraisal of the condition of the realm in this period is rare, especially in an official report. The document is key evidence of the extensive sacrifices that Louis XIV's policies were imposing upon his state even before the longest and costliest wars of his reign.

SOURCE. *Mémoires des intendants sur l'état des généralités dressés pour l'instruction du duc de Bourgogne*, A. M. de Boislisle, ed., Paris, 1881, Vol. I, pp. 781–786. Translated for this book by William F. Church. Published in 1881 by the Librairie Imperiale, Paris.

In the reports that we made concerning the salt tax and *aides* in the Orléanais and Le Maine, we noted the apparent abuses in the collection of these two *fermes*. We also noted the means whereby we thought it possible to remedy these abuses, either by improved administration or even by reducing certain royal rights[1] that seemed the most burdensome and the collection of which involved the greatest expense and trouble. But after examining with the greatest care the condition of the provinces that we visited by order of the king, we felt obliged to add, by means of this memorandum, that we found there a generally evil condition, much worse than any that might have resulted from the abuse of his majesty's rights and requiring remedies other than those that we recommended in the reports.

This evil is the poverty of the people. In all ages there are complaints against the needs of government and for this reason we were skeptical of the vague, general talk that we heard concerning the matter. But we were unable to remain unconvinced because of the specific facts that we observed and report herewith under certain heads.

One of the clearest evidences of the prosperity of a country is an increase in population whereas on the contrary its diminution is certain evidence of poverty. Now, we verified that the number of families has considerably declined almost everywhere, not counting those that left because of their religion. What became of them? Misery dispersed them. They went out to beg and perished in hospitals or elsewhere.

In the villages and the countryside one sees almost no games or diversions; everything languishes and is melancholy because pleasure and happiness are found only in the midst of prosperity, whereas the people hardly have the necessities of life. . . . In the villages where girls of a certain social standing were given doweries of 20,000 *livres*, they now receive hardly half that amount. . . . Houses that fall into ruin in the cities and villages are not repaired because their owners lack the necessary means. We saw many abandoned and destroyed in this way.

The number of taverns in the countryside is declining except

---

[1] The royal rights (*droits du roi*) were a series of miscellaneous levies, many of feudal origin, and were usually collected by tax farmers who administered the *fermes*. (Editor's note.)

at crossroads and only one or two are now found where there were four or five. Moreover, each of these earned more than those that remain.

There are hardly any peasants that own property. This is a great evil because a peasant who owns his land lives contentedly, cultivates it, and increases its value over that of his neighbors.

Another most grievous evil is that there are almost no well-to-do peasants. Earlier they were equipped and furnished with all necessities for improving their farms. They had cattle for plowing and manure; they had several farm-laborers; they could keep the wheat that they harvested and sell it when most advantageous. Today there are only poor small farmers who own nothing. The proprietors must furnish them with cattle, advance them money on which to live, pay their *tailles*, and take in payment the peasant's entire portion of the harvest. Even this is sometimes insufficient to cover his debts. Thus the small farmers earn nothing; they leave the land as destitute as they came to it. They can hardly afford a farm-laborer. Since the land is not well cultivated, it yields less. An illness, hailstorm, or a thousand other accidents to which these poor people are subject reduces them to beggary. The proprietors on their side are hardly in better position because these expenses, advances, and the wasting away of cattle that the peasants neglect because they do not own them consume all that the owners derive from their farms, without counting the losses that stem from the knavery of the wretches who sometimes sell the cattle and eat the proceeds. The result is that a man who formerly owned two or three well-maintained and cultivated small farms gives up one or two and contents himself with only one, adding to it all the land that constituted the others. This is the present state of husbandry in the countryside. It deserves careful consideration because agriculture should be one of the principal foundations of the sustenance and wealth of the people.

In the villages where oxen were killed to feed the inhabitants only cows are now slaughtered and the consumption of meat has greatly diminshed. This is even more evident in the countryside where the peasants live on bread made of buckwheat. Others who lack even this live on roots of ferns boiled with barley flour or oats and salt.

The price of cattle has greatly declined. In the fairs they are sold only in smaller quantities than is desirable because the peasants who bring in cattle are often obliged to return with them for lack of a buyer. It is the same with the price of wool, which has dropped by nearly one half.

But the peasants' extreme misery is more evident in their houses than anywhere else. We found them lying on straw; no clothes but the worthless ones on their backs; no furnishings; no provisions to support life. Everything indicated poverty.

Indeed, there is little basis for taxation and this causes the tax-collectors to be more circumspect. For they well know that if they burden the people and do not treat them with consideration, they will be reduced to the position of being able to pay nothing.

There are many fewer students in the schools than before because fewer parents are able to support the studies of their children. This is apparent in the large dioceses where it is becoming difficult to find priests.

The factories that brought much money to the areas where they were established and supported a great many people have considerably declined, both in the price of their products and their sales. Of those who worked there some have turned to begging and others can hardly subsist.

Finally, we observed in all classes and groups a noticeable contraction and an almost universal decline that requires prompt remedy. For regardless of the possibility that in a major crisis the people might no longer be able to furnish the necessary aid, it is greatly to be feared that even without any new burden matters will degenerate to the point where it will be most difficult to revive them, either as concerns the king's rights or the people's livelihood which should be regarded as inseparable.

We considered the counterargument, however, that the *fermes* have not declined and the royal rights have never been more promptly and peaceably paid than at present. Why then are the people so wretched? We must admit that this question gave us pause for a long time and caused us to doubt the truth of all that we had seen and heard. But after extensive reflection we found the proof of poverty in the manner in which royal rights are levied, for although the *fermes* have been maintained at the same level for several years, they do not rest on the proper foundations, that is, prosperity and expanding trade, but on increases in royal rights, more efficient collection, and other similar measures which are as new burdens on the people. Many examples illustrate this. . . .

In this way the *fermes* have been maintained but two conclusions are to be drawn. First, they effectively declined because they were supported in this manner. If they had remained essentially unchanged, the argument against all that we have said concerning the people's poverty would be almost unanswerable, but the increases that have been made indicate that the foundation is lacking and support is needed. It is a structure that is threatened with ruin and must be sustained with props. . . Second, these means of maintaining the *fermes* have been a burden on the people. If we continue to support them by such measures in the future, they may exhaust the provinces and consequently destroy the basis of the *fermes*. . . .

To return to the peoples' poverty, it is certain from all we saw that this is great, so much so that almost all the money in the provinces goes into paying royal rights. This is the sole object of work; it holds first rank and takes preference over the contract prices of the *fermes*, personal debts, and even necessities of life because of widespread, voluntary self-limitation and the profound respect in which everything that bears the name of his majesty is held. There is almost no money left for individuals; from this comes the decline of commerce and the proprietors' difficulties in securing income from their lands, especially in distant areas.

It is not difficult to understand the causes of this poverty and the scarcity of money. Although extraordinary levies and forced payments may have been necessary for the good of the state at the time when they were made, they nevertheless harmed or ruined those who were subject to them and many others. The extensive and repeated movements of soldiers that were needed for the execution of his majesty's projects and to maintain discipline among the troops were impossible to carry out without great cost to the inhabitants, no matter how well regulated. All that is taken from the provinces by the collectors and tax-farmers for the payment of levies and royal rights, and all that is taken by great lords, nobles, abbés, and others who live at the court, in the army, or in Paris and return less to the provinces draws away their wealth. The multiplication of lawsuits, charges by petty officials and justices, and the costs that are required to bring cases to trial contribute to the ruin of many persons. Finally, the decline of consumption and trade, the primary effect of the people's poverty, is self-perpetuating and increasing. These are among its most general and apparent causes that everyone sees.

It is similarly easy to understand its remedies. Two are necessary and essential: to relieve the people and to reestablish consumption and trade. There is nothing mysterious in these two measures and everyone understands them. This demonstrates their importance and necessity for there is no surer evidence of the truth of anything than general agreement by all.

It would be desirable to find means of restoring the people's wealth without lessening taxes and the income from the *fermes,* but this is impossible. Any expedients whatsoever will be fruitless unless the people are in condition to make use of them, and they cannot be brought to this point unless they are allowed to have the money with which to make purchases, trade, and carry on production. It is true that the king has granted a considerable reduction of the *tailles,* but in their exhausted condition the people have greater difficulty paying their present taxes than their earlier ones. The state is a weakened body from which small efforts now drain more than great ones did when it was in full vigor. It is therefore necessary to spare it and begin by rebuilding its strength. But this is not enough; consumption and trade must be reestablished. Lightening the burden will contribute something; suppression or reduction of certain royal rights will contribute much more. We assembled all that we learned of this matter in the provinces that we visited, and it is difficult to anticipate with certainty the success of any other measures. They require a superior and more extensive knowledge which, when consistently and generally applied to all parts of the state, always seeks what is appropriate to each and capable of restoring its prosperity. But the two aforenamed expedients are the only true means of solidly and lastingly supporting the *fermes;* all others are false and deceptive and only serve to worsen the evil rather than to cure it. They will cost something at first but the expense will later be repaid with interest. When consumption and trade are once reestablished, the king who has done many more difficult things will have the satisfaction of continually witnessing the growth of the people's happiness and his revenue in like proportion. Both will increase the strength of his state as well as his power and glory.

7   *Pierre Jurieu (?)*
            The Sighs of Enslaved France

The Soupirs de la France esclave *were published in Amsterdam as a series of memoirs during 1689 and 1690. Their author may have been Pierre Jurieu, one of the leading French Calvinist pastors who fled to Holland during the persecution of the Huguenots. In any case, they were the work of a French Huguenot in exile and were among the most famous of such tracts to be published abroad. The second memoir deals with the more important types of oppression by the French government and is translated here. In it, the author makes sweeping charges against Louis XIV's absolutism as responsible for the many ills of France. As so often in this period, the theme is excessive taxation and resulting misery. When the author claims that in France the king is everything and the state nothing, he overshoots the mark, since it is well known that Louis consistently devoted his energies to state building as he understood it. Whether the author's charges that all is sacrificed to Louis XIV's vanity and that his wars were unjustified are similarly exaggerated, the reader should judge. In any event, the* Soupirs *may be regarded as an expert presentation of the resentments against Louis XIV's rule that were sharply increasing during the latter part of the century.*

Having considered the oppression of the Church, the nobility, the Parlements, and the cities, we should examine that of the

SOURCE. *Les Soupirs de la France esclave, qui aspire après la liberté*, n.p., 1690, second memoir. Translated for this book by William F. Church.

people.[1] It must first be understood that under the present government, everyone is of the people. We no longer recognize quality, distinction, merit, or birth. The royal authority has risen so high that all distinctions disappear and all merit is lost. From the heights to which the monarch has been raised, all humans are but dust beneath his feet. By grouping all among the people, oppression and misery have been extended even to the noblest and highest elements of the state. This oppression of the people is caused primarily by the prodigious number of taxes and excessive levies of money that are everywhere taken in France. Taxes and finance are a science today, and one must be skilled to speak knowledgeably of them, but it suffices for us to relate what we all feel and what the people know of the matter. There are the personal and real *taille*. There are taxes on salt, wine, merchandise, principal, and revenue. This miserable century has produced a flood of names [of taxes], most of which were unknown to our ancestors or, if some were known, they were not odious because of the moderation with which they were imposed and levied. . . . It does not serve my purpose to acquaint you with the details of these taxes so that you may feel their weight and injustice. It will suffice to enable you to understand the horrible oppression of these taxes by showing (1) the immense sums that are collected, (2) the violence and abuses that are committed in levying them, (3) the bad use that is made of them, and (4) the misery to which the people are reduced.

First, dear unfortunate compatriots, you should realize that the taxes that are taken from you comprise a sum perhaps greater than that which all the other princes of Europe together draw from their states. One thing is certain, that France pays two hundred million in taxes of which about three-fourths go into the coffers of the king and the rest to expenses of collection, tax-farmers, officials, keepers, receivers, the profits of financiers, and new fortunes that are created in almost a single day. For the collection of the salt tax alone, there is a great army of officers and constables. Now I state as a fact and support it at the risk of my life that, except in time of war, the Kings of Spain,

---

[1] The French word *"peuple"* in seventeenth-century usage denoted the lower classes, that is, the peasantry and the city proletariat. (Editor's note).

England, Sweden, Denmark, the Emperor, and all the princes of
Germany and Italy, the Republics of Venice and Holland do not
take from their states two hundred million in ordinary taxes.
The thing is notorious, and I believe that no one will doubt it.
Note this well, I beg you, and consider whether there was ever
such a wasteful tyranny that went this far. . . .

If tyranny is clear and evident in the immense sums that are
levied in France, it is not less so in the manner of collecting
them. Kings were established by the people to preserve their
persons, lives, liberty, and properties. But the government of
France has risen to such excessive tyranny that the prince today
regards everything as belonging to him alone. He imposes taxes
at will without consulting the people, the nobles, the Estates,
or the Parlements. I shall tell you something that is true and that
thousands know but most Frenchmen do not. During Colbert's
ministry it was discussed whether the king should take immediate possession of all real and personal property in France and
reduce it to royal domain, to be used and assigned to whom-
ever the court judged appropriate without regard for former
possession, heredity, or other rights. In precisely the way that
the Moslem princes of Turkey and Persia and the Great Moghul
made themselves sole masters of all property, giving it to whom-
ever they pleased, but only for life. . . . I beg you to realize
where you are and under what type of government you live. . . .

How much abuse and violence is committed in the collection
of taxes? The meanest agent is a sacred person who has absolute
power over gentlemen, the judiciary, and all the people. A single
blow is capable of ruining the most powerful subject. They con-
fiscate houses, furnishings, cattle, money, grain, wine, and everything in sight. The prisons are full of wretches who are responsible for sums that they impose upon other wretches who cannot pay what is demanded of them. Is there anything more harsh
and cruel than the salt tax? They make you buy for ten or twelve
sous per pound something that nature, the sun, and the sea provide for nothing and may be had for two farthings. Under pretext of exercising this royal right, the realm is flooded with a
great army of scoundrels called constables of the gabelle who
enter houses, penetrate the most secret places with impunity,
and do not fail to find unauthorized salt wherever they think

there is money. They condemn wretches to pay huge fines, cause them to rot in prison, and ruin families. They force salt upon people everywhere and give each family more than three times as much as they can consume. In the provinces by the sea, they will not permit a poor peasant to bring home salt water; they break jugs, beat people, and imprison them. In a word, every abuse is committed in levying this and other taxes which is done with horrible expense, seizures, imprisonments, and legal cases before the collectors and courts with costs far above the sums involved. . . .

This is how all of France is reduced to the greatest poverty. In earlier reigns, that is, during the ministries of Cardinal Riche-lieu and Cardinal Mazarin, France was already burdened with heavy taxes. But the manner of collecting them, although not entirely just, nevertheless exhausted the realm much less than the way in which they are collected today. . . . The government of today has changed all of this. M. de Colbert made a plan to reform the finances and applied it to the letter. But what was this reformation? It was not the diminution of taxes in order to relieve the people. . . . He increased the king's revenue by one half. . . .

After this, if we examine the use that is made of these im-mense sums that are collected with such abuses and extortion, we shall find all the characteristics of oppression and tyranny. It sometimes happens that princes and sovereigns exact levies that appear excessive and greatly inconvenience individuals, but are required by what are called the needs and necessities of the state. In France there is no such thing. There are neither *needs* nor *state*. As for the *state*, earlier it entered into everything; one spoke only of the interests of the *state*, the needs of the *state*, the preservation of the *state*, and the service of the *state*. To speak this way today would literally be a crime of lese majesty. The king has taken the place of the state. It is the service of the *king*, the interest of the *king*, the preservation of the provinces and wealth of the *king*. Therefore the king is all and the state nothing. And these are no mere figures of speech but realities. At the French court, no interest is considered but the personal interest of the king, that is, his grandeur and glory. He is the idol to which are sacrificed princes, great men and small, families, provinces, cities, finances and generally everything. Therefore, it is not for the good of the state that these horrible exactions are made, since there is no more state. Neither are there *needs*. For France has never had fewer, except in the last few months. For thirty years, she has had no enemies but those that she light-heartedly made for herself. She might have lived in perfect peace. All the powers of Europe that might have offended her were weakened; thrones were occupied either by child princes or rulers with mediocre ability and pacific natures devoid of ambition. The Treaties of Münster and the Pyrenees had extended her frontiers and protected her former possessions by new peace settlements that had been conceded to her. Never had France lived in a time so favorable and so suitable for prosperous living and acquiring riches and power. On the contrary, never were her misery and bondage so sharply increased. Therefore, it was not to defend her and repel enemy invasions that her money was used.

This money is used solely to nourish and serve the greatest self-pride and arrogance that ever existed. It is so deep an abyss that it would have swallowed not only the wealth of the whole realm but that of all other states if the king had been able to take possession of it as he attempted to do. The king has caused himself to receive more false flattery than all the pagan demi-gods did with true flattery. Never before was flattery pushed to this point. Never has man loved praise and vainglory to the extent that this prince has sought them. In his court and around himself he supports a multitude of flatterers who constantly seek to outdo each other. He not only permits the erection of statues to himself, on which are inscribed blasphemies in his honor and below which all the nations of the earth are shown in chains; he causes himself to be represented in gold, silver, bronze, copper, marble, silk, in paintings, arches of triumph, and inscriptions. He fills all Paris, all his palaces, and the whole realm with his name and his exploits, as though he far surpassed the Alexanders, the Caesars, and all the heroes of antiquity. And all of this for having stolen three or four provinces from a weak, underage prince, for having known how to exploit the divisions within the Empire and the lack of understanding between its members, for having robbed a poor duke, for having purchased several important strongholds, and for having harrassed half of his own realm by persecuting Calvinism. To this the greatness of Louis the Great is reduced; it is a self-pride of immense proportions. And it is this enormous passion that devours so much wealth and to which so many sacrifices are made.

The immense revenues of the crown are used, first, for sumptuous buildings to glorify the king. No one will ever know the cost of Versailles. If it ever becomes known and is made public, no one will believe it. . . . The king's ancestors were not sufficiently well lodged. The Louvre, Fontainebleau, and Saint-Germain were too small to house such a prince. Something greater and more magnificent than all of these was required. So that the king's grandeur might appear to better advantage, it was necessary to build this magnificent palace in a place neglected by nature and to replace all that it lacked at enormous expense. It is a dry area, and to bring in water it was necessary to change the face of nature, create valleys where mountains had stood, raise water to new heights, change the course of rivers, and create pools and lakes in places where there had been only desert. Who can count the millions in gold that were consumed and the thousands of men that perished merely in working on the Eure River? Is it not a great pleasure for a state to feel its veins drained of their last drop of blood and its entrails torn out so as to erect eternal monuments to the vanity of the prince? Will it bring solid advantage to the realm some day to say of the work of Louis the Great: in this he consumed two or three hundred million, coerced nature, and buried more lead in the earth than is mined in several years? Or that he spared nothing in enriching it with marbles, decorations, paintings, rich furnishings, and precious jewels that were purchased and brought from the four corners of the earth? After all this, is there anyone who would regret losing the money, furnishings, and property that are wrenched from him through taxation?

Such a prince, so superbly lodged, cannot spend moderately in so great an establishment. That is why he must consume in banquets, officials, mistresses and their attendants, fortunes for their relatives, in celebrations, operas, comedies, ballets, apartments, presents to women and favorites, guards, and pensions two or three times as much as was formerly spent in maintaining the armies and strongholds on the frontiers of the state. Is this not good use of the realm's money? May one doubt that the king is everything and his pride the divinity to which all is sacrificed? . . .

Would you know another item of expenditure that consumes prodigious sums? It is the immense gifts that he makes to favorites so as to raise his creatures and set up new princes in the world. The house of Le Tellier probably possesses eighty or a hundred million, that of Colbert almost as much, and the others in proportion. There are French subjects that are much richer than several sovereigns of Europe, although the latter are very wealthy. If the state and its interests were the main concern, there could be no worse expenditures, for these newly great who rise from the dust and climb to places beside the throne serve merely to beat down and annihilate the ancient houses. These are the tyrants and bloodsuckers of the state. It would be much more useful to disseminate the wealth among the public than to allow it to be garnered by a single man. . . .

Let us now come to the expenses that seem most justified. The king spends endlessly on pensions. There is hardly a prince in Europe to whom he has not made himself tributary. And where he cannot gain the prince himself with money, he gains favorites, ministers, and often the princess who sleeps on the breast of the sovereign. He pays them fat pensions, gives them valuable presents, and by this means reigns everywhere. The king spends endlessly for armies and troops. In the midst of peace, he maintains more troops than the most bellicose of his ancestors supported during the most sanguinary wars. He makes war on his neighbors always to his advantage. In these wars he always drags enormous armies after him, but he has also extended the realm by five great provinces, Alsace, the Franche-Comté, Lorraine, Luxembourg, and Flanders, all of which constitute a realm and render France the terror of Europe. May expenditures be better utilized, and should one regret one's losses since the public gains so much? This expense, in fact, is well justified if one accepts the principle that is now followed at the court: *the prince is all, the people nothing, and all should be directed solely toward the grandeur of the king,* for certainly all this implements the cognomen, Great, that has been added to the name, Louis. But if instead of this false principle we assume the truth, which is that the good of the state and the public should be the supreme law, it will be found that what is called the glory of France is the greatest of evils because these conquests, from which we derive so much honor, are unjust, odious, and burdensome to the state. *They are unjust.* . . . Money is used to maintain numerous armies so as to carry on unjust wars that render the French name odious to all Europe and persuade others that France seeks universal monarchy and wishes to achieve it by means of infidelity, betrayal, violence, by breaking the most sacred peace treaties and conventions, by unheard-of barbarity, fire, and frightful desolation. Even if conquests were beneficial to us, should we purchase them at this price?

Moreover, who does not realize that conquests, instead of increasing the grandeur of the state, are burdensome and cause its ruin? We are mad, and our folly preserves our bondage. Whenever the king wins a battle, takes a city, or subdues a province, we light bonfires, and every petty person feels elevated and associates the king's grandeur with himself. This compensates him for all his losses and consoles him in all his misery. He does not realize that he loses as much as the king gains. First, the prince's grandeur always brings misery to his subjects, for the greater his power, the more he indulges his passions because he may more easily satisfy them. Now ambition, avarice, luxury, and waste are always the passions of the great. The more they are in position to exploit others, the more they do so. The subjects of a prince who has abundant crown lands, money, provinces, and arms are always the most wretched and oppressed. Consider how the people in the Orient live under the powerful Emperors of Turkey and Persia and the Great Moghul. It is therefore to the people's interest to limit the power of their king so that he cannot crush their liberty. Second, I would hope that the French who derive so much honor from the five or six provinces and more than two hundred strongholds that the king has conquered or built from Dunkirk to Basle would tell me at whose expense these provinces are held, kept, and maintained. These new subjects are lions and wolves tethered by the ears; they gnash their teeth and are always ready to devour us at the first opportunity. They abominate French domination and merely await the moment to cast off their yoke. Therefore, they must always be controlled. The fortresses that were found standing in these conquered provinces were insufficient; new ones were built everywhere in Flanders, on the Saar, the Rhine, and up to the gates of Basle. How many garrisons and governors must be maintained? I state as a fact that the king does not take from these conquered areas one-eighth of what is needed to hold them. Who furnishes the rest? Is it not the ancient domain of the crown, the older provinces? This is what is gained by Normandy, Brittany, Champagne, Guyenne, Languedoc, etc. They must find thirty or forty million to pay for the king's grandeur and preserve his conquests.

Finally, to be fully convinced how burdensome these new conquests are to the state, consider the jealousy of our neighbors. Even though our new subjects may become subdued and accustomed to obeying the king, will neighboring rulers willingly accept his possessing their wealth and ancient domains? Will they not fear that allowing him to keep what he has taken will give him the means of taking more? At the rate that the king has advanced for twenty years, France will become the mistress of all Europe. This is well understood and will always cause our neighbors to form leagues and plot our destruction. Even now you see the effect of this prediction. From whence comes this formidable league of all Christian princes who unanimously conspire to destroy us if not from their jealousy of the king's grandeur? France must therefore perpetually maintain great armies. And who will pay for them? It will not be the conquered areas. On the contrary, they will be favored so as to prevent their joining our enemies; moreover, they will be troubled enough because they will be theaters of war. Thus it is the ancient Kingdom of France that will bear the entire burden, even though it is already crushed by the weight of these new conquests. Such is the use that is made of the immense sums that are taken from you.

8   *Fénelon*
The Condition of the French Army

François de Salignac de la Mothe-Fénelon (1651-1715), Archbishop of Cambrai, was one of the ablest churchmen and theologians in France during the latter part of Louis XIV's reign. Fénelon won an international reputation for his great learning and for many years enjoyed high favor at the royal court, rivalling even Bossuet. Later he fell from Louis' good graces, largely because of intrigue. Being "exiled" to his archbishopric, he took his espiscopal duties seriously and became an excellent administrator. During the War of the Spanish Succession, the high respect in which he was held by all parties enabled him to travel through his diocese without molestation even when the area was overrun by the enemy. The English, Germans, and Dutch allowed him complete freedom of movement, and he was offered a military escort which he refused. For these reasons he was thoroughly conversant with conditions in northern France. This piece on the state of the French army in the north was written in 1710 and vividly portrays the exhaustion of the fighting forces and the realm generally during the final phases of the War of the Spanish Succession.

If I were to take the liberty of judging the condition of France by the portions of the government that I imperfectly see on this frontier, I would conclude that we survive only because of miracles and that the government is a delapidated machine that continues to run only on momentum and will collapse at the first shock. I would be tempted to believe that our greatest weakness is that no one perceives the essence of our condition; there even seems to be a desire to avoid seeing it. They do not dare face up to the exhaustion of our forces. Everything is reduced to blind grasping without knowing what is to be had; today's miracle only serves to answer for the one that will be needed

SOURCE. Fénelon, "Mémoire sur la situation déplorable de la France en 1710," *Oeuvres de Fénelon*, Paris, 1824, Vol. XXII, pp. 499–503. Translated for this book by William F. Church. Published in 1824 by L'Imprimerie de J. A. Lezel, Imprimeur du Roi.

tomorrow. They do not wish to perceive the facts and the extent of our ills and to take appropriate steps until it is too late.

This is what I see and intend to say constantly to the wisest and most informed persons.

The soldiers are often unpaid. Often they may even go several days without bread; it is made almost entirely of oats, badly cooked and full of dirt. These poorly nourished soldiers will fight badly, in all likelihood, and are heard to mutter and say things that should be alarming. The junior officers suffer proportionally even more than the soldiers. The majority, having exhausted all the credit of their families, eat the bad bread and drink the water of the camp. There are a great many of them who lack the means to return from their provinces; many others languish in Paris where they fruitlessly ask help of the minister of war. Others who are in the army are in a state of discouragement and despair that causes us to fear the worst.

The general of our army is unable to prevent disorder among the troops. Can one punish soldiers who are being made to die of hunger and who pillage only to avoid complete exhaustion? Do we wish that they not be in condition to fight? But on the other hand, how many evils are to be expected when they go unpunished! They ravage the whole countryside. The peasants fear the troops that should defend them as much as those of the enemy that seek to attack them. The army can hardly move from one position because it usually has bread for only one day. It is even obliged to remain near the area through which it may receive supplies, that is, Hainaut. It lives only on grain that comes to it from the Dutch.

Our fortifications, which we thought the strongest, have achieved nothing. In Menin and Tournai, we even saw that the king was deceived by their masonry, which was worthless. Every stronghold also lacks munitions. If we lose another battle, these places will fall like a house of cards.

The peasants no longer live like human beings, and it is impossible to count on their patience when it is put to such terrible tests. Those who lost their wheat, which was sown in the spring, have no other resources. Others, somewhat more remote, are also about to lose their wheat. Since they have nothing to hope for, they have nothing to fear.

The funds of all the cities are exhausted. Their revenues of ten years hence have been taken for the king, and demands are shamelessly being made, with threats, for new advances that are double those already taken. All the hospitals are filled to overflowing; they refuse the townsmen for whom they were built and are filled with soldiers. Great sums are owed these hospitals but instead of being paid, they are more overcrowded every day.

The French prisoners in Holland are dying of hunger for lack of payment by the king. Those who have had permission to come back to France dare not return to Holland, although they are honor bound to do so, because they cannot pay the cost of the journey or meet the debts that they owe in enemy territory.

Our wounded lack nourishment, linen, and medication. They cannot even find shelter because they are sent to hospitals that are already overcrowded by the king, entirely filled with injured soldiers. Who would risk being wounded in battle, knowing that he will neither be treated nor helped? Soldiers have been heard to say in their despair that if the enemy comes they will lay down their arms. We may judge from this what is to be expected of a battle that will decide the fate of France.

The whole province is damaged by confiscating wagons and killing the peasants' horses. This destroys the tillage for years to come and leaves neither peasants nor troops any hope of surviving. We may judge from this how odious French domination has become to the entire province.

In spite of themselves, the intendants ravage almost as much as the marauders. They steal even from public depots, openly deplore the shameful necessity that reduces them to this, and admit that they cannot keep the promises that they have been ordered to make. They cannot do their duty without cheating on all sides; it is the way of beggars rather than governors. The nation seems completely bankrupt. Notwithstanding violence and fraud, many important transactions must be abandoned whenever they cannot be carried out without advancing two hundred *pistoles* to meet the most pressing needs.

The nation is falling into disrepute and becoming an object of ridicule. Our enemies openly say that the Spanish government which we so despised never fell as low as ours. Our common people, soldiers, and officers no longer evince loyalty, respect, confidence, hope of rising again or fear of authority; everyone seeks only to evade the laws and wait for the end of the war regardless of its price.

If we lose a battle in Dauphiné, the Duke of Savoy will invade an area filled with Huguenots; he could raise several provinces of the realm in revolt. If we lose one in Flanders, the enemy will advance to the gates of Paris. What succor will remain? I know not. God grant that someone knows!

9   *Fénelon*
            Questions for the Royal Conscience

During his period of favor at the royal court, Fénelon was appointed tutor of the Duke of Burgundy, Louis XIV's grandson and heir to the throne. When Fénelon was later "exiled" to Cambrai, he remained in close touch with the Duke in spite of Louis XIV's disapproval of the relationship. At court, the Duke of Burgundy and some of his close associates, notably the Dukes of Beauvilliers and Chevreuse, were extensively influenced by Fénelon's political ideas, which contrasted strongly with both the theory and practice of Louis XIV's government. It was the hope of this group that Fénelon's ideal of monarchy, limited by legal tradition and Christian morality, would guide royal policy once the Duke of Burgundy ascended the throne. In retrospect, their hopes seem well founded since the Duke was apparently convinced along these lines and was expected by all to succeed his grandfather. The plan came to naught, however, when the Duke unexpectedly died in 1712.

Among Fénelon's several political writings, the Examen de conscience *is the most important statement of his political ideas. Although intended for the Duke of Burgundy's instruction and written in a manner designed to cause considerable soul-searching by this young man, the work was inevitably a critique of Louis XIV's reign. Throughout the treatise, it is clear that Fénelon constantly had in mind Louis' more questionable acts and was warning the heir to the throne against repeating them. Thus the work is an uncompro-*

SOURCE. Fénelon, "Examen de conscience sur les devoirs de la royauté," *Oeuvres de Fénelon*, Paris, 1824, Vol. XXII, pp. 266–269, 277–280, 284–291. Published in 1824 by L'Imprimerie de J. A. Lebel, Imprimeur du Roi. Also printed in *Fénelon, Ecrits et lettres politiques*, C. Urbain, ed., Paris, 1920. Translated for this book by William F. Church. Published by Editions Bossard, 43 rue Madame, Paris.

mising condemnation of Louis XIV's policies, which Fénelon found
to be diametrically opposed to the ideal of Christian monarchy and
the good of the people.

Do you sufficiently understand all the truths of Christianity?
You will be judged according to the Gospel like the least of your
subjects. Do you study your duties according to this divine law?
Would you permit a magistrate repeatedly to judge the common
people in your name without knowing your laws and ordinances,
which should be his standard of judgment? Do you hope that
God will permit you to ignore his law according to which He
desires that you live and govern his people? Do you read the
Gospel, not with idle curiosity but with humble docility, search-
ing for its practical meanings and directing your thoughts against
yourself so as to condemn yourself for everything that this law
rebukes in you? . . .

Have you never neglected to pray in order to ask God for
understanding of his will concerning you? Have you sought in
prayer the grace to profit from your reading? If you have
neglected to pray, you have rendered yourself guilty of all the
ignorance in which you have lived and which the spirit of prayer
would have removed from you. It means little to read eternal
truths if you do not pray for the gift of understanding them
thoroughly. Not having prayed well, you have merited the dark-
ness in which God has left you regarding the correction of your
faults and the accomplishment of your duties. Thus negligence,
indifference, and voluntary distraction in prayer, which usually
pass for the least of faults, are none the less true sources of the
ignorance and fatal blindness in which most princes live. . . .

Have you made the effort to instruct yourself in the laws,
customs, and usages of the realm? The king is the first judge in
his state. It is he who makes the laws, interprets them according
to necessity, and frequently judges in his council according to
the laws that he has made or those that were already established
before his reign. It is he who should correct all other judges. In
a word, his function is to lead the way in justice during peace
as it is to be at the head of his armies in war. But as war should
only be made regretfully, terminated as quickly as possible, and
waged in order to ensure a lasting peace, it follows that the func-

tion of military command is merely temporary, necessitated by circumstances and regretted by all good kings, whereas that of judging the people and keeping watch over all other judges is the natural, essential, and customary function of kings, inseparable from royalty. To judge well is to judge according to the laws; to judge according to the laws you must know them. Do you know them and are you qualified to correct judges who are ignorant of them? . . .

Have you never taken anything from one of your subjects by mere act of authority contrary to the laws? Have you reimbursed him as any individual should when you took his house, enclosed his field in your park, suppressed his office, or abolished his pension? Have you thoroughly examined the true needs of the state in comparison with the distress that taxes cause before imposing them on your people? Have you consulted with men who are most enlightened concerning this important question, most zealous for the public good, and most capable of telling you the truth without flattery or weakness? Have you never called a necessity of state something that served merely to flatter your ambition, such as a war for conquest and glory? Have you never called your own pretensions public necessities? If you have a personal claim to the succession of a neighboring state, you should support the resulting war with the income from your domain, your savings, and personal borrowing, but in any event without taking money from the people, except the help that they may give you because of pure affection, and without crushing them with taxes to support pretensions that do not interest them, for they will be no happier when you acquire another province. . . .

Have you sought means of relieving the common people and taking from them only what the true needs of the state require you to take for their advantage? The people's goods should be used only for the true benefit of the people themselves. You have your domain, which should be retired and liquidated; it is intended for the support of your household. You should reduce your domestic expenses, especially when the domain revenues are mortgaged and the people are exhausted. Taxes from the people should be used for the true expenses of the state. You should make every effort in time of public poverty to reduce all expenses that are not absolutely necessary. Have you consulted the most skillful and best intentioned persons who might inform you concerning the state of the provinces, the cultivation of the land, the size of recent harvests, the condition of commerce, etc., so that you may know what the state can pay without suffering? Have you regulated each year's taxes accordingly? Have you willingly listened to the remonstrances of upright persons? Instead of curbing them, have you sought them out and anticipated them as a good prince should? You know that in earlier times the king never took anything from the people merely by act of authority; it was the Parlement, that is, the assembly of the nation that granted him the sums needed for the extraordinary expenses of the state. Except in this instance he lived from his domain. What has changed this state of affairs if not the absolute authority that kings have taken? . . .

Have you never permitted levies of troops that were not entirely voluntary? It is true that the people are obligated to defend the state but only in wars that are just and absolutely necessary. You should choose young men in each village who are free, whose absence will not reduce husbandry, trade, or other necessary activities, and who have no families to support. You should thoroughly keep your promise to discharge them after a few years of service so that others will relieve them and serve in their turn. But to permit the levying of men by force, to cause a whole family that has been deprived of its head to languish and often to perish, to tear the laborer from his plow, keep him ten or fifteen years in service where he usually dies miserably in a hospital that lacks all necessities, to break his head or cut off his nose if he deserts—nothing can excuse this before God or man.

Do you take care to free each prisoner from the galleys at the end of the term that the court established for his punishment? The condition of these men is frightful; nothing is more inhuman than to prolong their terms. Never say that you would lack convict labor if you followed justice; justice is preferable to such labor. You should regard your true power only as that which you may wield without offending justice or taking anything that is not yours.

Do you give your troops the pay that is necessary to permit them to live without pillaging? If you do not, you clearly oblige them to commit the robbery and violence that you ostensibly prohibit. Do you punish them for doing what you well know they cannot refrain from doing and without which it would be necessary for them to abandon military service? On the other hand, do you neglect to punish them when they publicly commit thievery contrary to your prohibitions? Would you subject the laws to contempt and permit men to make light of your authority? . . .

Have you never committed injustice against foreign nations? A poor wretch who steals a coin on the highway in his great need is hanged but a man who make conquests, that is, who unjustly subjugates a province or a neighboring state, is treated as a hero! The theft of a field or vineyard is regarded as an unpardonable sin in the eyes of God unless it is returned but the theft of cities and provinces is counted as nothing! To take another's field is a great sin; to seize a province is an innocent and glorious act! Where are ideas of justice? Will God judge in this manner? "Thou thoughtest that I was altogether such a one as thyself."[1] Should the great be less just than the small? Is justice no longer justice when the greatest interests are involved? Are the millions of men who constitute a nation less our brothers than a single man? Should one not scruple to inflict upon millions of men or an entire province the injustice that one would not dare do for a single man's field? All that is taken by pure conquest is therefore acquired most unjustly and should be returned; all that is seized in a war that is undertaken for an unjust reason is the same. Peace treaties settle nothing when you are the strongest and reduce your neighbors to signing in order to avoid greater ills. In this case they sign like a man who gives his purse to a thief who holds a pistol to his throat. Far from satisfying your conscience, a war that you begin unjustifiably and pursue with success obliges you not only to return the conquered provinces but to compensate for all the injury that you caused your neighbors without reason. . . .

When contemplating war, have you first examined your rights with the aid of the most intelligent and least servile persons? Do you distrust the advice of certain ministers who have personal interests in involving you in war or who at least seek to flatter your passions so as to draw from you something to satisfy theirs? Have you sought out all arguments that might be contrary to

[1] Psalm L, 21.

yours? Have you listened favorably to those who would elaborate upon them? Have you given yourself the opportunity to learn the thoughts of the wisest counsellors without prejudicing them in advance?

Have you never regarded your personal glory as justification for embarking upon an enterprise for fear of passing your life without distinguishing yourself more than other princes? As if princes might find lasting glory by troubling the happiness of people whose fathers they should be! As if the father of a family might become praiseworthy by acts that make his children miserable! As if a king might hope for glory from other than his true virtue, that is, his justice and good government of his people! Have you never believed that war was necessary to acquire strongholds that were convenient to you or would ensure the safety of your frontiers? A strange rule! In following convenience, one would advance further and further until one reached China. The safety of a border may be secured without taking what belongs to others. Fortify your own strongholds but do not take those of your neighbors. Would you wish a neighbor to take everything from you that he thought convenient to his security? Your security is not a property title to the wealth of others. True security for you is to be just, to keep good allies by upright and moderate conduct, and to rule over a numerous, well-nourished, loving, and well-disciplined people. What is more contrary to your security than to cause your neighbors to feel that they can find none with you and that you are always ready to take from them anything that you find convenient?

Have you carefully examined whether a war might be necessary to your people? It may only be a question of some claim to a succession which concerns you personally; your people have no real interest in it. What is it to them if you acquire another province? Because of their affection for you if you treat them as a father should, they may make some effort to help you acquire the succession to states that legitimately fall to you. But should you burden them with taxes in spite of themselves in order to find the necessary funds for a war that brings them nothing? Moreover, even if the war concerns the state, you should examine whether it will be more advantageous or injurious; you must compare the gain that might result, or at least the loss that may be feared if it is not undertaken, with the disadvantages that it will entail.

All things considered, there is almost no war, not even a successful one, that does not bring more evil than good to a state. One has only to consider how many families it ruins, the number of men it causes to perish, how it ravages and depopulates the countryside, disrupts the state, degrades the laws, permits license, and how many years are required to repair the damage wrought by two years of war to good state policies. Would any intelligent and rational man enter upon the most legally justified lawsuit if he were certain that even in winning it he would do more harm than good to the large family for which he is responsible?

Comparison of the good and evil consequences of war should always persuade a good king to avoid war because of its disastrous consequences, for where are the profits that may counterbalance so many inevitable evils, not to mention the risk of failure? There is only a single case in which war is necessary in spite of all its evils; this is when one may avoid it only by permitting too great an advantage to an unjust, untrustworthy, and overly powerful enemy. In this instance, avoidance of war because of weakness would cause a state to decline even more dangerously. The resulting peace would not be a peace but only its false image. In this case it is necessary to prosecute war vigorously in spite of oneself because of one's desire for a good and firm peace. But this single instance is rarer than is commonly believed, and it is often thought to be real when it is only imaginary.

When a king is just, sincere, scrupulously faithful to his allies and powerful in his land because of wise government, he possesses the means of resisting attacks by his restless and unjust neighbors—his people's love and his neighbors' confidence. Everyone is interested in supporting him. If his cause is just, he has only to use the most lenient methods before resorting to war. Because he is already powerfully armed, he can afford to believe his neutral, disinterested neighbors, take upon himself certain burdens of peace, avoid all that may sharpen disputes, and try all roads to agreement. If all of these come to nothing, he can make war with greater confidence, since he will have God's protection, greater support from his subjects, and more aid from his allies. But it will very rarely happen that he is reduced to making war under these circumstances. Three-fourths of all wars occur because of pride, trickery, greed, or impetuosity.

COMMENTARIES

10   *Voltaire*
              Louis XIV: Builder of France

Voltaire, who was born François Marie Arouet (1694–1778), was not only the most famous philosopher of the Enlightenment but a historian of the first order. A pioneer in the writing of cultural history, he developed the concept that civilization owed its rise and development to certain great ages that made the major contributions to human betterment. Of these periods, the reign of Louis XIV was the most important, since it marked the triumph of rational philosophy. Voltaire was therefore very favorably inclined toward the rule of the Sun King, and this predilection was further strengthened by his admiration of personal absolutism which he interpreted as enlightened despotism. Although he criticized Louis XIV's record in certain areas, especially foreign affairs, Voltaire admired his handling of internal reforms and insisted that these were essentially the work of the king rather than his ministers. Voltaire was even sympathetic with Louis' thirst for glory, for he believed that "every king who loves glory loves the public weal." His analysis of Louis XIV's domestic reforms may be regarded as the classic statement of Louis' contribution to the building of France by a ruler who "did more good for his country than twenty of his predecessors together."

One owes this much justice to public men who have benefited their own age, to consider the point from which they started

SOURCE. Voltaire, *The Age of Louis XIV*, Martyn P. Pollack, tr., New York: E. P. Dutton, 1961, pp. 320–338. Everyman's Library edition. Reprinted by permission of E. P. Dutton & Co., Inc. Copyright 1921 by J. M. Dent & Sons, Ltd., London.

in order to perceive more clearly the changes they wrought in their country. Posterity owes them eternal gratitude for the examples they gave, even though such examples have been surpassed. Such lawful glory is their only reward. It is certain that the love of such glory inspired Louis XIV, at the time of his taking the government into his own hands, in his desire to improve his kingdom, beautify his court and perfect the arts.

Not only did he impose upon himself the duty of regularly transacting affairs with each of his ministers, but any well-known man could obtain a private audience with him and any citizen was free to present petitions and projects to him. The petitions were first received by a master of requests who wrote his recommendations in the margin; and they were then despatched to the ministerial offices. Projects were examined in council if they were thought worthy of such attention, and their authors were on more than one occasion admitted to discuss their proposals with the ministers in the king's presence. There was thus a channel between the throne and the nation which existed notwithstanding the absolute power of the monarch.

Louis XIV trained and inured himself to work; work which was the more arduous to him as he was new to it and the allurement of pleasures might easily distract him. He wrote the first despatches to his ambassadors. The more important letters were often revised by his own hand, and he made it a habit to read every document which bore his name.

Colbert had scarcely restored the finances of the country after the fall of Fouquet, when the king rescinded all the taxes owing for the years 1647 to 1658—in particular, three millions of polltaxes. Certain burdensome duties were removed by payment of five hundred thousand crowns a year. The Abbé de Choisi seemed thus much misinformed or very prejudiced when he said that the receipts had not decreased. They were undoubtedly decreased by such abatements and increased as a result of better methods of collection.

It was due to the efforts of the first president of Bellièvre, assisted by the benefactions of the Duchess d'Aiguillon and a few citizens, that the general hospital was founded. The king enlarged it and had others built in all the principal towns of the kingdom.

The great highways hitherto impassable were no longer neglected and became gradually what they are today under Louis
XV—the admiration of foreigners. Leaving Paris in any direction
one may now travel from fifty to sixty miles to various places
near at hand on well-paved roads bordered by trees. The roads
constructed by the ancient Romans were more lasting, but not
so wide and beautiful.

Colbert's genius was chiefly directed to commerce, which was
as yet undeveloped and whose fundamental principles were as
yet unknown. The English, and to a still greater extent the Dutch,
carried nearly all the trade of France in their ships. The Dutch
especially loaded up in our ports with French produce and
distributed it throughout Europe. In 1662 the king took steps to
exempt his subjects from a tax known as *freight duty*, which was
payable by all foreign ships; and allowed the French every facility
for transporting their own goods themselves at lower charges.
It was then that maritime trade sprang up. The council of commerce which is still in existence was established, and the king
presided over it every fortnight. Dunkirk and Marseilles were
declared free ports, a privilege which soon attracted the trade of
the Levant to Marseilles and that of the North to Dunkirk.

A West India company was formed in 1664 and an East India
company was established in the same year. Previous to this the
luxury of France had been entirely dependent upon the industry
of Holland. The supporters of the old system of economy, timid,
ignorant and narrow-minded, vainly declaimed against a system
of commerce by which money, which is imperishable, was continually being exchanged for perishable goods. They did not
reflect that these wares from the Indies, which had become indispensable, would have been much dearer if bought from a
foreign country. It is true that more money is sent to the East
Indies than is received from them, and that Europe is thus im-
poverished. But the bullion itself comes from Peru and Mexico,
being the price paid for our wares at Cadiz, and more of this
money remains in France than is absorbed by the East Indies.

The king gave more than six millions of present-day money
to the company; and urged wealthy people to interest themselves
in it. The queens, princes and all the court provided two millions

in the currency of the time, and the higher courts furnished twelve hundred thousand livres; financiers, two millions; the company of merchants, six hundred and fifty thousand livres. Thus the whole nation supported their ruler.

This company exists to the present day; for although the Dutch took Pondicherry in 1694 with the result that trade with the Indies declined from that time, it received a fresh impetus under the regency of the Duke of Orleans. Pondicherry then became the rival of Batavia, and this Indian company, founded under extremely adverse conditions by the great Colbert, re-established in our time by remarkable efforts, was for some years one of the principal resources of the kingdom. In 1669 the king also formed a Northern company; he contributed to its funds as to the Indian company. It was then clearly shown that there is nothing derogatory in trade, since the most influential houses took an interest in such establishments, following the example of their monarch.

The West India company was no less encouraged than the others, the king supplying a tenth part of the total funds.

He gave thirty francs for every ton exported and forty for every ton imported. All who built ships in national ports received five livres for every ton of carrying capacity.

One cannot be too much astonished that the Abbé de Choisi should have condemned these institutions in his *Memoirs*, which must not be relied upon. We perceive to-day all that Colbert in his capacity as minister did for the good of the nation, but it was not perceived at the time; he worked for ungrateful people. Paris resented his interference in suppressing certain revenues of the town hall acquired very cheaply since 1656, and the fall in the value of bank-notes, which had been lavishly poured out under the preceding ministry, much more than it appreciated what he had done for the common good. There were more merchants than good citizens. Few persons had any views on the public welfare. It is well known how private interests blind the eyes and cramp the mind; I am speaking not only of the interests of a merchant, but those of a company, those of a town. The rude answer given by a merchant, named Haxon, when consulted by Colbert, was still widely quoted in my youth: "You found the carriage overturned on one side and you have upset it on the other"; and this anecdote is to be found in Moreri. It was left for the spirit of philosophy, introduced at a very late period into France, to amend the prejudices of the people, before complete justice could be at length accorded to the memory of that great man. He had the same exactitude as the Duke de Sulli and possessed much wider views. The one could merely organise, the other could build up great institutions. After the Peace of Vervins, the only difficulty Sulli had to overcome was the maintenance of a rigid and strict economy; Colbert was obligated to provide at a moment vast resources for the wars of 1667 and 1672. Henri IV assisted Sulli with his economy reforms, while the extravagance of Louis XIV continually thwarted Colbert's efforts.

Nevertheless, there is little that was not either re-established or created in his time. In 1665, visible proof of a liberal circulation was forthcoming when the interest on the loans of the king and private individuals was reduced to five per cent. He wanted to enrich France and increase her population. People in the country were encouraged to marry by exempting those who had done so by the age of twenty from paying poll-tax for a period of five years; and every head of a family of ten children was exempt for the remainder of his life, since he gave more to the state by the product of his children's work than he would have done by paying taxes. Such a law should never have been repealed.

Each year of this ministry, from 1663 to 1672, was marked by the establishment of some manufacture. Fine stuffs, which had hitherto come from England and Holland, were now manufactured at Abbeville. The king advanced to the manufacturer two thousand livres for each loom at work, in addition to considerable grants. In the year 1669 there were 44,200 wool looms at work in the kingdom. Fine silk manufactures produced more than fifty millions in the currency of the time, and not only were the profits much greater than the outlay on the necessary silk, but the growing of mulberry trees enabled the manufacturers to dispense with foreign silk for the weaving of their material.

In 1666 glass began to be made as fine as that of Venice, which had hitherto supplied the whole of Europe, and soon French glass attained a splendour and beauty which have never been surpassed elsewhere. The carpets of Turkey and Persia were excelled at *La Savonnerie*. The tapestries of Flanders yielded to those of *Les Gobelins*. At that time more than eight hundred workmen were employed in the vast Gobelin works, and three hundred of them were actually lodged there; the finest painters directed the work, which was executed either from their designs or copied from those of the old Italian masters. It was in the precincts of the Gobelins that inlaid work was also produced—a delightful kind of mosaic work—and the art of marquetry was brought to perfection.

Besides the fine tapestry factory at *Les Gobelins* another was established at Beauvais. The first manufacturer in the town employed six hundred workmen, and the king made him a present of sixty thousand livres. Sixteen hundred girls were employed in making lace; thirty of the best operatives in Venice were engaged, and two hundred from Flanders; and they were presented with thirty-six thousand livres to encourage them.

The manufactures of Sedan cloth and of Aubusson tapestry, which had deteriorated and dwindled, were again set going. Rich stuffs, in which silk was interwoven with gold and silver, were made at Lyons and Tours, with a fresh outburst of industry.

It is well known that the ministry bought from England the secret of that ingenious machine by which stockings can be made ten times more quickly than with the needle. Tin, steel, fine crockery-ware, morocco leather, which had always been brought from foreign countries, were now worked in France. But certain Calvinists, who possessed secrets of tin and steel smelting, carried them away with them in 1686, and shared them and many others with foreign nations.

Every year the king bought about eight hundred thousand livres' worth of works of art, manufactured in his kingdom, and gave them away as presents.

The city of Paris was very far from being what it is to-day. The streets were unlighted, unsafe and dirty. It was necessary to find money for the constant cleaning of the streets, for lighting them every night with five thousand lamps, completely paving the whole city, building two new gates and repairing the old ones, keeping the permanent guard, both foot and mounted, to ensure the safety of the citizens. The king charged himself with everything, drawing upon funds for such necessary expenses. In 1667 he appointed a magistrate whose sole duty was to superintend the police. Most of the large cities of Europe have imitated these examples long afterwards, but none has equalled them. There is no city paved like Paris, and Rome is not even illuminated.

In every sphere matters tended to become so perfect that the second-lieutenant of police in Paris earned a reputation in the performance of his duties which placed him on a level with those who did honour to their age; he was a man capable of anything. He was afterwards in the ministry, and would have made a good general in the army. The position of second-lieutenant of police was beneath his birth and capabilities; yet in filling that post he earned much greater reputation than when occupying an uneasy and transient office in the ministry towards the end of his life.

It should be here pointed out that M. d'Argenson was not by any means the only member of ancient chivalry who performed the office of a magistrate. France is almost the only country in Europe where the old nobility has so often donned the robe. Nearly all other countries, swayed by a relic of Gothic barbarism, are unaware of the greatness of this profession.

From 1661 the king was ceaseless in his building at the Louvre, Saint-Germain and Versailles. Following his example private individuals erected thousands of dwellings in Paris as magnificent as they were comfortable. Their number increased to such an extent that in the environs of the *Palais-Royal* and *St. Sulpice* two new towns sprang up in Paris, both vastly superior to the old. It was about this time that those magnificent spring carriages with mirrors were invented, so that a citizen of Paris could ride through the streets of that great city in greater luxury than the first Roman triumvirs along the road to the Capitol. Inaugurated in Paris, the custom soon spread throughout the whole of Europe, and, become general, it is no longer a luxury.

Louis XIV took delight in architecture, gardens, and sculpture, his delight being for all that was grand and imposing. From 1664 the Comptroller-General Colbert, who was in charge of buildings, a duty properly belonging to the ministry of arts, devoted himself to the carrying out of his master's plans. The Louvre must first be finished, and François Mansard, one of the greatest French architects of all time, was chosen to construct the immense buildings that had been projected. He declined to proceed, unless he were allowed to alter certain parts already built which appeared to him defective. These doubts he cast on the scheme, to alter which would have entailed too great an expense, were the cause of his services being dispensed with. The cavalier Bernini was summoned from Rome, famous already for the colonnade surrounding the parvis of St. Peter's, the equestrian statue of Constantine, and the Navonna fountain. An equipage was provided for his journey. He was brought to Paris as a man come to do honour to France. He received, in addition to the five louis a day for the eight months he remained, a present of fifty thousand crowns and a pension of two thousand, and five hundred for his son. This generosity of Louis XIV towards Bernini was yet greater than the munificence accorded to Raphael by Francis I. In gratitude Bernini afterwards cast at home the equestrian statue of the king which now stands at Versailles. But once arrived in Paris with so much pomp as the only man worthy to work for Louis XIV, he was not a little astonished to see the design of the façade of the Louvre on the Saint-Germain-l'Auxerrois side, which when finished shortly afterwards became one of the most imposing architectural monuments to be found in the world. Claude Perrault was the draughtsman, and it was executed by Louis Levau and Dorbay. He invented machines for conveying the stone blocks, fifty-two feet long, which form the pediment of this majestic building.

Men sometimes seek very far afield for what they have at home. Not a Roman palace has an entrance comparable to that of the Louvre, for which we are indebted to that Perrault upon whom Boileau dared to try to pour ridicule. In the opinion of travellers, those famous *vineyards* are not comparable to the *Château de Maisons,* which was built at such small cost by François Mansard. Bernini was magnificently remunerated, but did not deserve his rewards: he merely drew up plans which were never executed.

After building the Louvre, the completion of which is greatly to be desired, founding a town at Versailles close to the palace which cost so many millions, building Trianon, Marli, and beautifying so many other buildings, the king had completed building the Observatory, begun in 1666, at the time that he founded the Academy of Sciences. But the work glorious for its utility, its vastness and the difficulties of its construction, was the Languedoc canal, which connected the two seas, and finds an outlet in the port of Cette, built for that purpose. All these undertakings were begun after 1664 and were continued uninterruptedly until 1681. The founding of the Invalides and its chapel, the finest in Paris, the building of Saint-Cyr, the last of the edifices to be erected by that monarch, would alone suffice to hallow his memory. Four thousand soldiers and a large number of officers, who find consolation in their old age and relief for their wounds and needs in the former of those great institutions; two hundred and fifty girls of noble birth who receive in the latter an education worthy of their high position, are so many witnesses to the glory of Louis XIV.

The institution of Saint-Cyr will be surpassed by the one which Louis XV is about to found for the education of five hundred noblemen, but so far from causing Saint-Cyr to be forgotten, it will remind one of it; the art of doing good is thus brought to perfection.

Louis XIV resolved at the same time to do greater things, of more general utility as they were more difficult of accomplishment, and one of these was the remodeling of the laws. He instructed the chancellor Séguier, Lamoignon, Talon, Bignon and, above all, the state councillor, Pussort, to set to work. He was sometimes present at their meetings. The year 1667 marked the epoch of his earliest statutes as it did his earliest conquests. The civil code appeared first to be followed by the law of rivers and forests, and later statutes concerning every kind of manufacture; the criminal code, the laws of commerce and the marine laws were passed in annual succession. A new kind of justice was even introduced in favour of the negroes in French colonies, a people who had not hitherto possessed the rights of mankind.

A sovereign need not possess a profound knowledge of juris-prudence; but the king was well versed in the principal laws; he entered into their spirit, and knew when either to enforce or modify them as occasion demanded. He often passed judgment on his subjects' law-suits, not only in the council of the state secretaries, but in that one bearing the name of the *council of the parties*. Two judgments of his have become famous, in which he decided against himself.

The first case, which was tried in 1680, was an action between himself and certain private individuals in Paris who had erected buildings on his land. He gave judgment that the houses should remain to them with the land belonging to him, which he made over to them.

The other one concerned a Persian, named Roupli, whose merchandise had been seized by the clerks of his farms in 1687. His decision was that all should be returned to him, and he added a present of three thousand crowns. Roupli carried back to his own country his admiration and gratitude. When the Persian ambassador, Mehemet Rixabeg, came afterwards to Paris, it was discovered that he had long known of that action by the fame which it had spread abroad.

The suppression of duelling was one of the greatest services rendered to the country. Formerly such duels had been sanctioned by kings, even by parliament and by the Church, and though forbidden since the days of Henri IV, the pernicious practice was more prevalent than ever. The famous combat of the La Frettes in 1663, when eight combatants were engaged, determined Louis XIV to pardon such duels no longer. His well-timed severity gradually reformed the nation and even neighbouring nations, who conformed to our wise customs after having copied our bad ones. At the present day the number of duels in Europe is a hundred times less than in the time of Louis XIII.

Legislator of his people, he was no less so of his armies. It is astonishing that before his time the troops had no uniform dress. It was he who in the first year of his administration decreed that each regiment should be distinguished by the colour of their uniform, or by different badges—a regulation which was soon adopted by all other nations. It was he who organised the brigadiers and gave the king's household troops the status they hold at the present day. He formed a company of musketeers from Cardinal Mazarin's guards and fixed the number of men for the two companies at five hundred, whom he furnished with the uniform they still wear to-day.

During this reign the post of High Constable was abolished, and after the death of the Duke of Epernon there were no more colonels-general of infantry; they were too much the master; he resolved to be the only master, and deserved to be so. Marshal Grammont, a mere colonel in the French guards under the Duke d'Epernon, and taking his orders from this brigadier-general, now only took them from the king, and was the first to bear the title of colonel of the guards; Louis himself appointed these colonels to the head of their regiments, presenting them with his own hands a gold gorget with a pike, and afterwards a spontoon, when the use of pikes was abolished. In the king's regiment, which is of his creation, he founded the grenadiers, at first to the number of four to each company; afterwards, he formed a company of grenadiers in each infantry regiment, and provided the French guards with two of them; at the present day there is one in every infantry battalion in the army. He greatly enlarged the corps of dragoons and gave them a brigadier-general. Nor must be forgotten the institution of breeding-studs in 1667. Heretofore, they had been absolutely neglected, and they were of great assistance in providing mounts for the cavalry; an important resource which has since been too much neglected.

The use of the bayonet attached to the end of the musket originated with him. Before his time they were sometimes employed, but only a few of the regiments fought with this weapon. There was no regular practice and no drill, all being left to the will of the general. Pikes were considered to be the most formidable weapon. The Fusiliers, founded in 1671, were the first regiment to employ bayonets and to be drilled in the use of that weapon.

The use to which artillery is put at the present day is entirely due to him. He established schools at Douai, and later at Metz and at Strasburg, and the artillery regiment found itself at last provided with officers who were nearly all capable of efficiently conducting a siege. All the magazines in the country were well stocked and eight thousand hundredweights of powder were distributed amongst them every year. He formed a regiment of bombardiers and hussars; before his time hussars were only to be found among the enemy.

In 1688 he established thirty militia regiments, furnished and equipped by the communes. These regiments were trained for war, but they did not neglect the tilling of the land.

Companies of cadets were maintained at most of the frontier towns; they were taught mathematics, drawing, and all manner of drill, and carried out the duties of soldiers. This system was pursued for ten years. At length the difficulties in the way of training insubordinate youths proved too great; but the corps of engineers, formed by the king and for which he drew up regulations which still obtain, will last for ever. Under Louis XIV the art of fortifying towns was brought to perfection by Marshal Vauban and his pupils, whose works surpassed those of Count Pagan. He constructed or rebuilt one hundred and fifty fortresses.

For the maintenance of military discipline, he created inspectors-general, and afterwards superintendents, who reported on the condition of the troops, and their reports showed whether the commissaries had carried out their duties.

He founded the Order of Saint Louis, and this honourable distinction was often more sought after than wealth itself. The Hôtel des Invalides crowned the efforts he made to be worthy of the faithful service of his subjects.

It was by such efforts that, from the year 1672, he possessed one hundred and eighty thousand regular troops, and increasing his forces proportionately to the increase in the number and power of his enemies he had at length as many as four hundred and fifty thousand men under arms, including the marines.

Before that time no such powerful armies had been seen. His enemies were able to put in the field armies almost as large, but to do so their forces were compelled to be united. He showed what France could do unaided, and had always, if not great success, at any rate great resources.

He was the first to give displays of war manœuvres and mimic warfare in times of peace. In 1698 seventy thousand troops were mustered at Compiègne. They performed all the operations of a campaign, the display being intended for the benefit of his three grandsons. The luxurious accompaniments of this military school made of it a sumptuous fête.

He was as assiduous in his efforts to secure the sovereignty of the seas as he had been to form numerous and well-trained armies upon land, even before war was declared. He began by repairing the few ships that Cardinal Mazarin had left to rot in the ports. Others were bought from Holland and Sweden, and in the third year of his government he despatched his maritime forces in an attempt to take Jijeli on the coast of Africa. In 1665 the Duke of Beaufort began to clear the seas of pirates, and two years later France had sixty warships in her ports. This was only a beginning, but while in the midst of making new regulations and fresh efforts, he was already conscious of his strength, and would not allow his ships to dip their flag to the English. It was in vain that King Charles II's council insisted on this right, which the English had acquired long since by reason of their power and labours. Louis XIV wrote to his ambassador, Count d'Estrades, in these terms: "The King of England and his chancellor may see what forces I possess, but they cannot see my heart. I care for nothing apart from my honour."

He only said what he was determined to uphold, and in fact the English surrendered their claims and submitted to a natural right and Louis XIV's firmness. Equal conditions obtained between the two nations on the seas. But while insisting upon equality with England, Louis maintained his superiority over Spain. By reason of the formal precedence conceded in 1662, he compelled the Spanish admirals to dip their flag to his ships.

Meanwhile the work of establishing a navy capable of upholding such arrogant sentiments progressed everywhere. The town and port of Rochefort were built at the mouth of the Charente. Seamen of all classes were enrolled, some of whom were placed on merchant vessels and others distributed among the royal fleets. In a short time sixty thousand were enrolled.

Building commissions were set up in the ports so that ships

might be constructed on the best possible lines. Five naval arsenals
were built at Brest, Rochefort, Toulon, Dunkirk and Hâvre-de-
Grâce. In 1672, there were 60 ships of the line and 40 frigates.
In 1681, there were 198 ships of war, counting the auxiliaries
and 30 galleys in the port of Toulon, either armed or about to be
so; 11,000 of the regular troops served on the ships, and 3000
on the galleys. 166,000 men of all classes were enrolled for the
various services of the navy. During the succeeding years there
were a thousand noblemen or young gentlemen in this service,
carrying out the duties of soldiers on board ship, and learning
everything in harbour to do with the art of navigation and tac-
tics; they were the marine guards, having the same rank at sea
as the cadets on land. They had been formed in 1672, but in
small numbers; they have since proved themselves a school which
has produced the finest ships' officers in the navy.

As yet no officer in the marine corps had been made a Marshal
of France, a proof that this vital part of France's forces had
been neglected. Jean d'Estrées was made the first marshal in 1681.
It seems that one of Louis XIV's great objects was to stir up
rivalry for this honour in all classes, without which there is no
initiative.

The French fleets held the advantage in every naval battle
fought until the engagement of La Hogue in 1692, when Count
de Tourville, obeying the orders of the court, attacked with
forty ships a fleet of ninety English and Dutch ships; he was
forced to yield to superior numbers and lost fourteen ships of
the first class, which ran aground and were burnt in order to
prevent them falling into the enemy's hands. In spite of this set-
back the naval forces still held their own; but they deteriorated
during the war of the succession. Subsequently Cardinal Fleury
neglected to repair their losses during the leisure of a prosperous peace—the very time in which to re-establish them.

The naval forces greatly assisted in protecting trade. The
colonies of Martinique, San Domingo and Canada, hitherto languishing, now flourished, and with unhoped-for success; for from
1635 to 1665 these settlements had been a burden upon the nation.

In 1664, the king established a colony at Cayenne and soon
afterwards another in Madagascar. He sought by every means

to redress the folly and misfortunes which France had brought upon herself by ignoring the sea, while her neighbours were founding empires at the ends of the world.

It will be seen by this cursory glance what great changes Louis XIV brought about in the state; and that such changes were useful since they are still in force. His ministers vied with each other in their eagerness to assist him. The details, indeed the whole execution of such schemes was doubtless due to them, but his was the general organisation. There can be no shadow of doubt that the magistrates would never have reformed the laws, the finances of the country would not have been put on a sound basis, nor discipline introduced into the army, nor a regular police force instituted throughout the kingdom; there would have been no fleets, no encouragement accorded to the arts; all these things would never have been peacefully and steadily accomplished in such a short period and under so many different ministers, had there not been a ruler to conceive of such great schemes, and with a will strong enough to carry them out.

His own glory was indissolubly connected with the welfare of France, and never did he look upon his kingdom as a noble regards his land, from which he extracts as much as he can that he may live in luxury. Every king who loves glory loves the public weal; he had no longer a Colbert nor a Louvois, when about 1698 he commanded each comptroller to present a detailed description of his province for the instruction of the Duke of Burgundy. By this means it was possible to have an exact record of the whole kingdom and a correct census of the population. The work was of the greatest utility, although not every comptroller had the ability and industry of M. de Lamoignon of Baville. Had the comptroller of every province carried out the king's intent so well as the magistrate of Languedoc with regard to the numbering of the population, this collection of records would have been one of the finest achievements of the age. Some of them are well done, but a general scheme was lacking since the same orders were not issued to each comptroller. It is to be wished that each one had given in separate columns a statement of the number of inhabitants of each estate, such as nobles, citizens, labourers, artisans, workmen, cattle of all kinds, fertile, mediocre, and poor land, all clergy, both orthodox and secular, their revenues, and those of the towns and communes.

In most of the records submitted all these details are confused; the matter is not well thought out and inexact; one must search, often with great difficulty, for the needed information such as a minister should have ready to hand and be able to take in at a glance so as to ascertain with ease the forces, needs and resources at his disposal. The scheme was excellent, and had it been methodically carried out would have been of the greatest utility.

The foregoing is a general account of what Louis XIV did or attempted to do in order to make his country more flourishing. It seems to me that one can hardly view all his works and efforts without some sense of gratitude, nor without being stirred by the love for the public weal which inspired them. Let the reader picture to himself the condition to-day, and he will agree that Louis XIV did more good for his country than twenty of his predecessors together; and what he accomplished fell far short of what he might have done. The war which ended with the Peace of Ryswick began the ruin of that flourishing trade established by his minister Colbert, and the war of the succession completed it.

Had he devoted the immense sums which were spent on the aqueducts and works at Maintenon for conveying water to Versailles—works which were interrupted and rendered useless—to beautifying Paris and completing the Louvre; had he expended on Paris a fifth part of the money spent in transforming nature at Versailles, Paris would be in its entire length and breadth as beautiful as the quarter embracing the Tuileries and the Pont-Royal; it would have become the most magnificent city in the world.

It is a great thing to have reformed the laws, but justice has not been powerful enough to suppress knavery entirely. It was thought to make the administration of justice uniform; it is so in criminal cases, in commercial cases and in judicial procedure; it might also be so in the laws which govern the fortunes of private citizens.

It is in the highest degree undesirable that the same tribunal should have to give decisions on more than a hundred different customs. Territorial rights, doubtful, burdensome or merely troublesome to the community, still survive as relics of a feudal government which no longer exists; they are the rubbish from the ruins of a gothic edifice.

We do not claim that the different classes of the nation should all be subject to the same law. It is obvious that the customs of the nobility, clergy, magistrates and husbandmen must all be different, but it is surely desirable that each class should be subject to the same law throughout the kingdom; that what is just or right in Champagne should not be deemed unjust or wrong in Normandy. Uniformity in every branch of administration is a virtue; but the difficulties that beset its achievement are enough to frighten the boldest statesman. It is to be regretted that Louis XIV did not dispense more readily with the dangerous expedient of employing tax-farmers, an expedient to which he was driven by the continual advance drawings he made on his revenues, as will be seen in the chapter on finance.

Had he not thought that his mere wish would suffice to compel a million men to change their religion, France would not have lost so many citizens. Nevertheless, this country, in spite of the shocks and losses she has sustained, is still one of the most flourishing in the world, since all the good that Louis XIV did for her still bears fruit, and the mischief which it was difficult not to do in stormy times has been remedied. Posterity, which passes judgment on kings, and whose judgment they should continually have before them, will acknowledge, weighing the greatness and defects of that monarch, that though too highly praised during his lifetime, he will deserve to be so for ever, and that he was worthy of the statue raised to him at Montpellier, bearing a Latin inscription whose meaning is *To Louis the Great after his death.* A statesman, Don Ustariz, who is the author of works on the finance and trade of Spain, called Louis XIV *a marvel of a man.*

All these changes that we have mentioned in the government and all classes of the nation inevitably produced a great change in customs and manners. The spirit of faction, strife and rebellion which had possessed the people since the time of Francis II, was transformed into a rivalry to serve their king. With the great landowning nobles no longer living on their estates, and the governors of the provinces no longer having important posts at their command, each man desired to earn his sovereign's favour alone: and the state became a perfect whole with all its powers centralised.

It was by such means that the court was freed from the intrigues and conspiracies which had troubled the state for so many years. There was but a single plot under the rule of Louis XIV which was instigated in 1674 by La Truaumont, a Norman nobleman, ruined by debauchery and debts, and aided and abetted by a man of the House of Rohan, master of the hounds of France, of great courage but little discretion.

The arrogance and severity of the Marquis de Louvois had irritated him to such a point that on leaving him one day he entered M. Caumartin's house, quite beside himself, and throwing himself on a couch, exclaimed: "Either Louvois dies . . . or I do." Caumartin thought that this outburst was only a passing fit of anger, but the next day, when the same young man having asked him if he thought the people of Normandy were satisfied with the government, he perceived signs of dangerous plans. "The times of the Fronde have passed away," he told him; "believe me, you will ruin yourself, and no one will regret you." The chevalier did not believe him, and threw himself headlong into the conspiracy of La Truaumont. The only other person to enter into the plot was a chevalier of Préaux, a nephew of La Truaumont, who, beguiled by his uncle, won over his mistress, the Marquise de Villiers. Their object and hope was not and could not have been to raise a new party in the kingdom; they merely aimed at selling and delivering Quillebeuf into the hands of the Dutch and letting the enemy into Normandy. It was rather a base and poorly contrived piece of treachery than a conspiracy. The torture of all the guilty parties was the only result of this senseless and useless crime, which to day is practically forgotten.

The only risings in the provinces were feeble disorders on the part of the populace, which were easily suppressed. Even the Huguenots remained quiet until their houses of worship were pulled down. In a word, the king succeeded in transforming a hitherto turbulent people into a peace-loving nation, who were dangerous only to their foes, after having been their own enemies for more than a hundred years. They acquired softer manners without impairing their courage.

The houses which all the great nobles built or bought in Paris, and their wives who lived there in fitting style, formed schools of gentility, which gradually drew the youth of the city away from the tavern life which was for so long the fashion, and which only encouraged reckless debauchery. Manners depend upon such little things that the custom of riding on horseback in Paris tended to produce frequent brawls, which ceased when the practice was discontinued.

Propriety, due in large part to the ladies who gathered circles of society in their *salons*, made wits more agreeable, and reading in the long run made them more profound. Treason and great crimes, such as bring no disgrace upon men in times of sedition and intrigue, were now hardly known. The enormities of the Brinvilliers and the Voisins were merely passing storms in an otherwise clear sky, and it would be as unreasonable to condemn a nation for the notorious crimes of a few individuals, as it would be to canonise a people for the reforms of a La Trappe.

Hitherto all the various professions could be recognised by their characteristic failings. The military and the youths who intended to take up the profession of arms were of a hot-headed nature; men of law displayed a forbidding gravity, to which their custom of always going about in their robes, even at court, contributed not a little. It was the same with university graduates and with physicians. Merchants still wore their short robes at their assemblies and when they waited upon ministers, and the greatest merchants were as yet but unmannerly men; but the houses, theatres, and public promenades, where everyone began to meet in order to partake of more refined pleasures, gradually gave to all citizens almost the same outward appearance. It is noticeable at the present day, even behind a counter, how good manners have invaded all stations of life. The provinces in time also experienced the effects of these changes.

We have finally come to enjoy luxury only in taste and convenience. The crowd of pages and liveried servants has disappeared, to allow greater freedom in the interior of the home. Empty pomp and outward show have been left to nations who know only how to display their magnificence in public and are

ignorant of the art of living. The extreme ease which obtains in
the intercourse of society, affable manners, simple living and the
culture of the mind, have combined to make Paris a city which, as
regards the harmonious life of the people, is probably vastly
superior to Rome and Athens during the period of their greatest
splendour.

These ever-present advantages, always at the service of every
science, every art, taste or need; so many things of real utility
combined with so many others merely pleasant and coupled with
the freedom peculiar to Parisians, all these attractions induce a
large number of foreigners to travel or take up their residence
in this, as it were, birthplace of society. The few natives who leave
their country are those who, on account of their talents, are
called elsewhere, and are an honour to their native land; or they
are the scum of the nation who endeavour to profit by the consideration which the name of France inspires; or they may be
emigrants who place their religion even before their country,
and depart elsewhere to meet with misfortune or success, following the example of their forefathers who were expelled from
France by that irreparable insult to the memory of the great
Henri IV—the revocation of his perpetual law of the Edict of
Nantes; or finally they are officers dissatisfied with the ministry,
culprits who have escaped the vigorous laws of a justice which
is at times ill-administered, a thing which happens in every
country in the world.

People complain at no longer seeing that pride of bearing at
court. There are certainly no longer petty autocrats, as at the
time of the Fronde, under Louis XIII, and in earlier ages; but
true greatness has come to light in that host of nobles so long
compelled in former times to demean themselves by serving over-
powerful subjects. To-day one sees gentlemen, citizens who
would formerly have considered themselves honoured to be
servants of these noblemen, now become their equals and very
often their superiors in the military service.

The more that services rendered are accounted above titles of
nobility, the more flourishing is the condition of the state.

The age of Louis XIV has been compared with that of Augustus. It is not that their power and individual events are comparable; Rome and Augustus were ten times more considered

in the world than Louis XIV and Paris, but it must be remembered that Athens was the equal of the Roman Empire in all things whose value is not dependent upon might and power.

We must also bear in mind that there is nothing in the world to-day to compare with ancient Rome and Augustus, yet Europe taken as a whole is vastly superior to the whole of the Roman Empire. In the time of Augustus there was but a single nation, while at the present day there are several nations, all civilised, warlike, and enlightened, who cultivate arts unknown to the Greeks and Romans; and of these nations, there is none that has shone more brilliantly in every sphere for nearly a century, than the nation moulded to a great extent by Louis XIV.

11   *Georges Pagès*
The Insufficiencies of Absolutism

Georges Pagès (1867–1939) was one of the ablest French historians of his generation. His interests lay primarily in institutional history, but he approached the field in a broad manner and was very learned in others. The book from which the present selection is taken was his most important work of synthesis and sets forth an interpretation of Louis XIV's reign that has had wide acceptance among French scholars during the nineteenth and twentieth centuries. Apparently originating with Lemontey early in the nineteenth century, it is to be found in the monumental work of Lavisse and has been continued, with modifications, in the publications of Mousnier. Thus it occupies a major place in the historical literature concerning French absolutism. Briefly, the view emphasizes the impact of institutionalized absolutism upon French society as a new type of despotism in many areas of human experience. This increased effective royal power but gave it no roots in the nation and, in combination with Louis XIV's

SOURCE. Georges Pagès, *La Monarchie d'ancien régime en France* (*De Henri IV à Louis XIV*), Paris: Librairie Armand Colin, 1932, pp. 182–203, 214–215. Translated for this book by William F. Church. Reprinted by permission of Librairie Armand Colin. Copyright 1927 by Max Leclerc et Cie.

shortsighted policies, alienated opinion and undermined the monarchy so extensively as to prepare the way for its eventual destruction. From this standpoint, French absolutism had outlived its usefulness long before the death of the Sun King.

From its beginnings the monarchy of the old regime had been absolute and sanctioned by divine right; it was more than ever thus under Louis XIV. Monarchical doctrine, carried to its furthest limits, became a type of dogma. To discuss it was heresy; to attack it was an offense against both human and divine law. This is what was meant by the well-known statement, "No matter how bad a prince may be, revolt by his subjects is always utterly criminal." In this sense the development of the monarchical principle had been carried to completion. We may, however, examine it from another standpoint. Until that time the monarchy had suffered from the instability and insecurity from which absolute power escapes only by renouncing despotism, that is, limiting itself. It was this type of renunciation that the Parlement had sought to impose upon the king when obliging him to recognize and respect the "fundamental laws" of the realm. But recognition of these fundamental laws would have changed the entire body of privileges, the basis of social organization, into inviolable public liberties. This seemed incompatible with the principle of absolutism. In Louis XIV's eyes, the spirit of the *Fronde* was not merely one of indiscipline and rebellion but the very negation of divine right monarchy. As much as Colbert and much more than his predecessors, Louis XIV felt a need for order that may have stemmed from his own nature and perhaps the influence of Cartesianism in French thought and which, in any case, tempered his despotism. We can hardly imagine Louis XIV living as Louis XIII, Richelieu, and Mazarin had earlier, in a continually provisional state and constantly resorting to expedients. Louis XIV readily maintained and it even seemed to give him pleasure that an administration might be organized so as to function according to fixed rules, provided that it acted in his name. More than any other king he merited the title that no medal in the *Histoire métallique* accorded him and which Lemontey first gave him, "Louis the Administrator."

But without foreseeing its consequences he thereby inaugurated a new era, for the ruin of the old regime is present in embryo in the institutions of Louis XIV's epoch. Simultaneously combining pure, personal absolutism and administrative growth, the monarchy of Louis XIV persisted only because of a precarious equilibrium that was soon broken. Its dissolution began to appear as early as the second half of the reign.

Actually, this was rendered inevitable by the great length of the reign. The accession of a new sovereign who participates in the spirit of his times facilitates the needed adaptation of institutions to changes in ideas and manners. During the fifty-four years of Louis XIV's personal rule, on the contrary, customs and ideas changed, society evolved, and the supports of divine-right monarchy weakened, but the government, far from making allowances for these developments, became more absolute and personal year after year.

The history of the "ministry" throughout the reign is very instructive in this respect. At Mazarin's death, Louis XIV was limited to choosing his ministers from the small number of men who were already in office and whose earlier services guaranteed their skill and fidelity. In this way he chose Michel Le Tellier, Lionne, and Colbert, choices that he never had occasion to regret. But however adaptable these three might be, their experience was too rich and their personal value too great for them to be mere instruments in the hands of their master. We must not be deceived by official writings such as the memoirs of the king. In 1661, from the end of April to the beginning of December, Louis XIV was at Fontainebleau. The queen was also there as were the ladies-in-waiting and La Vallière. Is it rash to assume that at twenty-three years of age the young king gave somewhat more time to his pleasures than he did at a later date and that without relaxing his authority he willingly gave over to his ministers the daily cares of government? He became accustomed to listening to their suggestions that were advantageous to his glory. In this way the influence and prestige of the "triad" were made clear to the public which was not deceived. In 1667, Saint-Maurice, the envoy of the Duke of Savoy, correctly assessed the situation in a letter of May 27. "On Sunday morning the ministers departed, and the circumstance that was most gratifying to all Paris and the most discerning minds was that they travelled together in the same carriage to Colbert's home. . . . All sorts of benefits are expected from their cooperation, perspicacity, zeal and knowledge."

Louis XIV appreciated their services. In spite of the pride that the adulation of the entire court nurtured in him, his mind was too upright for him not to retain his esteem and gratitude for Colbert. His letters give evidence of this. After several years, however, he began to show impatience at having permitted any minister, even a Colbert, to appear indispensable. To Colbert he therefore opposed Louvois whose favor increased after 1667. Soon he developed a system of dividing the ministry between these two families whose rivalry he simultaneously fostered and restrained. He called Louvois to the ministry in 1672; then from 1679 to 1683 the division was equal. The Supreme Council included four ministers, two Colberts, Jean-Baptiste and his brother, the Marquis of Croissy, and two Le Telliers, Michel and his son, the Marquis of Louvois. But once again a strong personality imposed itself upon the king without his resenting it at first. Le Tellier was aging; Croissy, although skillful, had little authority; Colbert, too discerning not to recognize the king's mistakes and too desirous of preserving his work to ignore them, became obtrusive. When he died in 1683, his son, Seignelay, was only Secretary of State for the Navy and did not participate in the Supreme Council. Into it Louvois introduced Le Pelletier who was thoroughly devoted to Louvois and received the office of Superintendent of Buildings. It was Louvois' advice and not Croissy's that impelled Louis XIV toward his policy of usurpation and violence which resulted in war against almost all of Europe in 1688. By means of his ascendancy over the king's mind, toward 1690 Louvois far surpassed Colbert's earlier influence and had "if not the sole, at least the principal part in directing great matters," as Spanheim wrote. Without straining the paradox one may speak of the "reign" of Louvois.

He disappeared in his turn in 1691 at the moment when the disastrous results of his policies were becoming apparent and when Louis XIV, over whom Madame de Maintenon watched in the background, began to reassert himself. Then seemed to occur the revenge of the Colbert family but now without the great Colbert and under the auspices of the conservative religious faction. In addition to Seignelay who became a minister in 1689 and died soon thereafter, Louis XIV called a son-in-law of Colbert to the ministry, the Duke of Beauvillier. But henceforth it was no longer the personalities of the ministers that counted. Neither Beauvillier, Pontchartrain, Chamillart, Desmarets, Voysin, nor even Torcy could aspire to play the role of a Colbert or a Louvois. After 1691, during the final twenty-four years of the reign, personal government such as Louis XIV had conceived in 1661 became more and more a reality. More than ever Bossuet could admire "this immense people united in a single person, a hidden mind concealed in a single head and governing the entire body of the state."

But at the same time another change was taking place and militated in the opposite direction, although this was not apparent at first. This was the growth of bureaucratic centralization. The government, although as personalized as a government can be, was also (as has often been said) one of commissioners and bureaus. It was by developing the bureaucracy that the Secretaries of State at the center and the intendants throughout the realm established their power and the latter became, as John Law wrote a little later, the "thirty Masters of Requests sent to the provinces, on whom depended their success or misfortune, their prosperity or sterility."[1]

At first the Secretaries of State themselves managed their departments, receiving almost daily orders from the king concerning various matters. As aids they had only two or three clerks apiece; their bureaus which were still undeveloped (and about which we know almost nothing) were located in Paris even when the court resided at Saint-Germain or Fontainebleau. But when the king undertook to administer his realm, the number of matters for which the Secretaries of State were answerable increased while the Council of Dispatches, where they might have been discussed, met only once a fortnight. This meant that Louis XIV dissociated himself from the council. Only the most important matters or those that directly concerned it were sub-

---

[1] On the Masters of Requests, see page oo, Note 1. (Editor's note.)

mitted to it by the Secretaries of State and were the subjects of officially approved decrees. Disposition of all other matters including current ones henceforth belonged to the Secretaries of State in person or, more frequently, their bureaus which sent them completed orders to be signed. When the court and the government were installed at Versailles, the bureaus grew to such proportions that they alone filled two long buildings on each side of the Great Court or Court of the Ministers. Modern bureaucracy was born and henceforth would have a life of its own, apart from the king.

The intendants naturally became its instruments in the provinces, but they also changed character. At first they had been chiefly investigators. They still left to the financial officials, treasurers, and *élus* certain remnants of their former administrative activity, and Colbert reminded them of the limits of their competence. They had hardly any bureaus. They made use of subdelegates which was nothing new, since the judicial intendants of Louis XIII's time had already done so, but Colbert permitted this practice only in exceptional cases when the press of affairs obliged the intendants to secure help. In 1674 he ordered the suppression of all permanent subdelegates, but he was not obeyed. At the end of the reign the intendants' competence had immeasurably increased. They henceforth were required to concern themselves with everything, intervene everywhere, and handle so many matters that they were quite obliged to rely upon the advice of their subordinates, that is, their bureaus which developed like those of the Secretaries of State, and their subdelegates who alone were able to obtain accurate local information and were established in all important cities of the intendancy. In each Generality the intendants succeeded each other without a break and transmitted their powers from one to the other; each administered only one such area rather than two or three as frequently happened before 1666. A consistent administration was created whose activity is well known through the great publications of Boislisle. It received the king's orders directly from the general office of control, but distance and the slowness of couriers allowed it wide initiative and in a given locality there was hardly any restraining influence upon it. From this time forward it created its own precedents and administrative regulations, which became its traditions. It was this that the subjects obeyed; it was for its benefit that local officials were dispossessed. As much as the king and perhaps even more, it was the administration that henceforth represented the state to the mass of the nation.

For the subjects of Louis XIV this was something entirely new. Although we know little of the daily life of local communities during the first half of the seventeenth century, we do know, as I have said, that they managed their own affairs. The king's authority was felt only intermittently. At lengthy intervals troops might appear to suppress a rebellion; more frequently the agents of the *fermes* came to establish or collect a tax. The latter, it goes without saying, were detested and their appearance almost always provoked violence or uprisings but the agents were not associated with the king; the inhabitants merely regretted that he was not rich enough to get along without the tax-collectors' services or strong enough to prevent their exactions. At the end of the century, on the contrary, the intendant's interference in municipal life was continual; in 1683 an ordinance brought local communities under his tutelage. By this means the cities were no doubt better administered; the intendant eliminated abuses and the common people gained thereby but the municipal oligarchy lost in the process and was incensed. Even the lower classes, accustomed as they were to their ills and respectful of the traditional hierarchy, often bore a grudge against this stranger who mixed into their affairs. "As if it pleased me to be down-trodden!" The phrase was then current. It was the intendants' administration that acquainted the nation with royal *despotism*. Was the alliance between the king and the middle class therefore broken? Not yet. But it is certain that the new administrative organization weakened it. We must also note, with Lemontey, the contradiction (which Colbert certainly did not perceive) in suppressing municipal independence at the precise moment when the government sought to develop large-scale industry and foreign commerce and for this purpose appealed to the spirit of enterprise of the bourgeoisie. Here also was manifest the contradiction between divine right absolutism and the evolution of modern society.

It was even more ominously apparent relative to the continued existence of a whole social class, the nobility, whose costly uselessness became a heavy burden upon society at the same time that it was a danger to the monarchy. But it seems that neither Louis XIV nor Colbert foresaw the consequences of this. A half century earlier, Richelieu in his *Testament politique* had sought means of making the nobility useful to the state. Louis XIV seems to have been satisfied with depriving them of any active role in the government as well as the nation. He drew the great nobility to Versailles but reserved for them only the honor of serving him, appearing in all the ceremonies of the royal "cult," and forming the sumptuous setting of his life; he carefully excluded them from his councils. In the provinces, the nobles hardly counted any longer beside the intendants. It was the intendant alone who oversaw the regulation of markets, effected the distribution of grain, lessened the burden of the *taille* on parishes that had been ravaged by hailstorms, and made arbitrary assessments on well-to-do persons who were subject to the *taille* but escaped these general levies and caused their weight to fall more heavily upon the poor. The peasants no longer looked to the lord to ease their burdens but to the intendant. As for the nobles whose tenant farmers paid as much as any others and sometimes more, they were increasingly reduced to idleness that rapidly resulted in poverty. It has been proved that the "reformations of the nobility" ordered by Colbert for the benefit of the treasury chiefly struck the nobles who *derogated* by participating in industrial and commercial enterprises in order to live. The nobles were limited to cultivating their farms that custom exempted from the *taille* and harshly exploiting their seigneurial rights, but the latter, which no service by the nobles justified, consequently seemed heavier to the tenants and the gulf between peasants and nobles widened. The nobility had only one honorable remaining function, war; they therefore clamored for it as though the king would have been remiss in one of his duties by not giving them the opportunity to fight. But they merely sought diversion in their idleness rather than wealth, for the price of officers' commissions was so high and life in the field so costly that their pay and bounties did not cover their expenses. How many nobles fought in the king's service until old age and finally returned, decorated with the Order of Saint-Louis but wounded and crippled, to die destitute in their ruined country-seats!

It was one of the irreparable mistakes of Louis XIV to have deliberately rendered the nobles useless. Lavisse correctly emphasized this. The result was not merely that they became odious to the nation but that the king, by surrounding himself with his nobility at Versailles, seemed to make common cause with them. At the same time that the evolution of customs and the economy was tending to fuse social classes, their traditional hierarchy became more than ever one of the fundamental laws of the realm. Royal power thus deprived itself of any basis but privilege. Henceforth the nobility and the monarchy of the old regime were bound one to the other and were destined to perish together.

The religious policy of Louis XIV contributed even more to preparing the ruin of the monarchy of the old regime. In order to calculate its consequences, we must consider its different elements.

First, his policy toward the Protestants. We do not know how many Protestants there were in France about 1661 nor even whether their number had increased or diminished during the period of governmental toleration that lasted from the Peace of Alais until Mazarin's death. At most, we may assume that Calvinism had ceased to spread because religious peace was in itself favorable to the larger and stronger Catholic Church and because even at that time neither the clergy nor the militant lay Catholics had ceased to combat the pretended reformed religion. But we know somewhat better how the Protestants were distributed throughout society. There were some in the army among whom their most glorious leader, Turenne, was not converted until 1668. Some were in the navy, including Duquesne, who refused to convert even after the Edict of Fontainebleau. There were some among the officers of the judiciary, the lawyers, and practitioners. There were many among the financial officials and even more among the masters of the guilds, the shipowners, and merchants in the seaports. They constituted only a minority, no doubt, but were rich, intelligent, active, and their influence upon opinion was not negligible. During the *Fronde* their loyalty had prevented the spread of the revolt, especially in southern France. Regarding the origins of royal power they adhered to the same theories as the Catholics and, almost until the eve of the Revocation, they maintained their respect for royal commands.

After 1661, however, successive edicts and declarations almost annually imposed new restrictions on the rights that the Edict of Nantes had seemingly guaranteed the Protestants. The result was not only increased curbs upon them; the repetition of restrictive measures, each foreshadowed by the previous one, angered and unnerved them. They were not duped by the sophistry of those who wrote commentaries on the edict, pretending to assure its strict execution by suppressing abuses, and the repeated requests of the Assembly of the Clergy showed them only too clearly the objective that the Catholic Church assigned royal policy. To fear of the future was thus added an awareness of injustice and hypocrisy. How could their loyalty remain intact? It wavered after 1680. After 1685 it gave way to feelings of indignation and then of hate that were only too justified by the dragonades, the kidnapping of converted children seven years old, the Protestants' sufferings in the galleys, and the incessant persecution of the new Catholics. Some of their enemies such as Basville, the intendant of Languedoc, understood this so thoroughly that they seemed to excuse them. "We must," he wrote in 1698, "regard the Protestants as an angered people who, . . . being persuaded that they have been done an injustice by denying them, contrary to the terms of the edict, that which men naturally regard as most free and dear, believe that they should in their turn abandon fidelity and patience."

The Revocation therefore created in the realm *an angered people* whose loyalty to their faith ranged them against their king. In upper Languedoc where sermons in the "desert" kindled exaltation, the anger of the mountain dwellers of the Cévennes reached the point of rebellion; the Camisards resisted the royal armies for many years. Outside France a focus of hate arose not far from her borders in Holland where most of the exiled pastors gathered. The most fanatic among them compared the king with the beast of the Apocalypse or called him and the pope anti-Christ. After the Glorious Revolution in England, all the pastors predicted to him the fate of James II and sought the restoration of their church only through the victory of the coalition. Jurieu served William III against Louis XIV. To the Catholics, of course, the Protestants henceforth appeared as rebels and their cause was compromised. In 1686 Bayle had vigorously protested against the Revocation in his *Commentaire philosophique sur les paroles du Christ: Contrains-les d'entrer.* He certainly was not suspected of sympathy for the persecutors. He nevertheless wrote in 1690 his *Avis aux réfugiés*, which caused a violent reaction in Amsterdam. But what did the apparently numerous new Catholics within the realm think, those who, unlike their brothers, had not had the courage to go into exile or refuse to abjure? Without doubt many were tortured by remorse, accused themselves of sacrilege, waited for God to deliver them however unworthy, and secretly hoped for the victory of the coalition. Louis XIV did not succeed in exterminating Protestantism; it took refuge in the desert or was hidden in the recesses of many hearts, ready to reappear in the open as soon as persecution was relaxed. But the Edict of Fontainebleau had the result (among many others) of profoundly dividing the nation and reviving the spirit of revolt. It renewed the danger, momentarily averted by the Edict of Nantes, of a division of consciences within a divine-right monarchy in which the union of the ancient church and royalty was indissoluble.

A division among *Catholic* consciences was bound to be even more dangerous to the *Catholic* monarchy of Louis XIV, yet this was the result of the persecution of the Jansenists. Its beginnings had appeared somewhat earlier than Louis XIV's personal rule, but it seems certain that this policy was determined by the king himself and not Mazarin who allowed the Formulary[2] to lie dormant after 1655. During these years three men dominated Louis XIV's mind: Father Annat, his confessor; Pierre de Marca, Archbishop of Toulouse; and the Archbishop of Rouen, Harley

---

[2] The Formulary was a statement repudiating five propositions that the royal censor claimed to have found in the *Augustinus*, a book by Jansenius, and were declared to be heretical by papal constitutions in 1653 and 1656. The Jansenists agreed that the propositions were heretical but denied that they were in the *Augustinus*. To accept the Formulary under these conditions amounted to an equivocation. (Editor's note.)

de Chanvallon who initiated the persecution in his diocese as early as 1660. At the same time the *Petites écoles* of Port-Royal were definitively dispersed. Then on March 9, 1661, Louis XIV created the Council of Conscience, associating with Father Annat two docile prelates who quickly succeeded each other in the See of Paris, Marca and Péréfixe who was Bishop of Rodez and former preceptor of the king. Finally in April the residents and novices in the two houses of Port-Royal were expelled and signature of the Formulary was demanded throughout the realm. The struggle against Jansenism was entirely the personal work of Louis XIV who gloried in it and doubtless hardly foresaw either its long duration or its far-reaching repercussions.

The latter were many, and one cannot exaggerate their importance. The principal one was not that a new minority of malcontents arose alongside the minority of Protestants, that of the persecuted Jansenists. The majority of the latter always remained good Frenchmen and royalists, and the attitude of the Great Arnauld in Belgium was very different from that of Jurieu in Amsterdam. The Jansenists did not blame the king but only the courtier-bishops who flattered him and especially his confessor. Their hatred, or more accurately their indignation, was entirely directed against their original enemies, the Jesuits, whom they accused of destroying morality, corrupting the Church, and introducing false doctrines into it by causing Saint Augustine to be condemned under the pretext of condemning Jansenius. There was moreover a great danger in this revival of hostility against the Jesuits at the moment when the king gave over to them the guidance of his conscience and made, as Fénelon said, his Jesuit confessor a minister.

Even more dangerous were the consequences of the controversies that henceforth perpetually agitated the Church. These were concerned with more than dogma. If the Jansenists and Jesuits had merely disputed concerning grace, they would have excited only a small number of theologians and pious laymen whose quarrels would at most have embarrassed the king in his relations with Rome but would not have imperilled the authority of the sovereign or the security of the state. But these disciples of Saint Augustine and Molina also discussed the guidance of consciences as well as morality and its foundations, and we are familiar with the reverberations that Pascal's *Lettres provinciales* caused when they appeared. The same happened later at the time of Quesnel when Richer's ideas that were favorable to the lower clergy penetrated Jansenism and brought into question the discipline and even the organization of the Church. At this point the court and the city-dwellers became interested in the controversy, eagerly followed its vicissitudes, and took sides in the quarrel. An unusual danger, this appeal to opinion in an area where authority had heretofore been exercised without limit. If the faithful were sufficiently emboldened to criticize the constitution of the Church, could the subjects long refrain from criticizing that of the state?

Besides, the persecution of the Jansenists offended or disturbed many more consciences than the persecution of the Protestants. I do not refer to the violence against the little band at Port-Royal but rather the Formulary. Signing of it was demanded of all clergy, regular and secular, and all who were immediately or remotely dependent upon the Church; it was a significant portion of the nation. They not only found themselves obliged to choose between their innermost scruples and their obedience to the twin authorities of bishop and king. The royal declaration of 1664 specified rigorous penalties for refusal to sign: no one might be received into holy orders or appointed to a benefice without having signed the Formulary. As for clerics who refused to sign, the benefices that they held were considered vacant and were conferred upon others. When one recalls that a considerable portion of the bourgeoisie then entered the Church because it provided them with means of livelihood as well as a decent and honored career, one will understand the discontent and anxiety that such legislation caused. It risked discouragement of many a calling and troubled even those that it did not touch. It injured and threatened a whole social class and brought into question the purposes that were associated with the lives of a great many upright persons and satisfied both their interests and their beliefs. In this regard, we can do no better than repeat what Rebelliau said of the Formulary. "The more we understand the specifics of religious life in France during the seventeenth and eighteenth centuries, the better we will realize the evil that the application of this agnostic and brutal instrument of pacification did to the French Church (and I would readily add the monarchical state). The seeds of disruption and revolt that it spread especially among the second order of the clergy, the most numerous, the entire eighteenth century brought to flower."

"Especially among the second order of the clergy." These few words prompt us to emphasize a final consequence of Louis XIV's religious policy and perhaps not the least momentous. Until that time, the monarchy of the old regime had linked its fortunes with those of the Church, but a national Church, the Gallican Church which almost unanimously supported the crown against the pretensions of the Holy See. The last striking manifestation of this union was the famous Declaration of Four Articles of 1682. But already the situation had changed and would change even more during the latter part of the reign. Since the Council of Trent, monarchical structure had thoroughly predominated in the organization of the Church Universal, and the popes, with the aid of the Jesuits, had endeavored to benefit from all its logical consequences. They strongly maintained the preeminence of the Roman See over all other sees and, contrary to the doctrine of the Councils of Constance and Basel, denied the superiority of a general council over the papacy. They already claimed infallibility in dogma, which was not made a law of the Church until the Vatican Council of 1870. These pretensions menaced both the authority of national churches and the independence of the bishops, and this is why Louis XIV and the General Assembly of the Clergy of France were united in protesting against such claims. But the General Assembly was not all the clergy; mere priests, in fact, were excluded from it during the latter part of the reign. Regarding them the *first order* of the clergy taught a doctrine very similar to that of the pope concerning the bishops. The latter did not wish to associate the *second order* with the government of the diocese and no longer assembled diocesan synods in which the priests had a place and might deliberate. Moreover, the bishops refused to admit that like themselves the priests had received by divine appointment the right to preach, receive confessions, and administer certain sacraments; they regarded the priests as mere delegates to whom authority given by the ordinary was indispensable for accomplishing all the acts of their sacred ministry. Now, toward the end of the seventeenth century, the will to resist began to awaken among the lower clergy; the ideas of Richer, although condemned earlier and rejected by the first Jansenists, were taken up again by a new generation whose most illustrious representative was Quesnel. Certain passages in his *Reflexions morales sur le Nouveau Testament* were characteristic in this respect, such as this one which invokes the tradition of the primitive Church. "Like their holy predecessors and the Good Shepherd who seem to have been willing to receive advice from their disciples, and like the Apostles who, far from begrudging their inferiors the role that they should have in making decisions and governing the Church, associated them with these things, the good bishops remained united with their priests."

Two contrary tendencies therefore appeared in the bosom of the Gallican Church. One was monarchical and sought to concentrate all the power in the diocese in the hands of the bishop as the pope was doing within the Church Universal. The other, which may be called democratic, claimed for the second order of the clergy and sometimes even the entire body of the faithful an important role in episcopal government. Of these two tendencies, it was difficult for Louis XIV not to favor the first; it was too consonant with the very principle of divine right monarchy. Well before the latter part of the reign he sided with it. When he established the capitation in 1695, the General Assembly of the Clergy agreed to an annual extraordinary payment of four million whereupon he granted it an Edict Regulating Ecclesiastical Jurisdiction. In the future no priest, secular or regular, was permitted to preach, receive confession, or administer the sacrament of penance without obtaining from the ordinary a special authorization, which the bishop might limit or revoke at any time without even stating his reasons. Soon after, in 1698, another edict permitted the bishop to order any priest into retreat in a seminary for a maximum of three months without indicating his motives. Besides, when this disguised suspension was insufficient, an easily obtained *lettre de cachet* always made possible a more rigorous penalty against an overly independent priest.

Several protests were made but were condemned by the General Assembly in 1700. Henceforth the bishops' authority, sustained by that of the king, was wielded without restraint until the end of the reign. More than ever the king allied himself with the prelates against the second order which was humiliated and angered, a fateful alliance that would contribute toward even further separation of the high and low clergy and the spreading among the vicars and priests of democratic ideas as dangerous to monarchy as to episcopacy. Some of the most momentous consequences of the religious quarrels of the eighteenth century were present in embryo at the end of the seventeenth in the profound discontent of the lesser clergy, and Louis XIV's government was more responsible for this than the bishops' pride.

Anxiety concerning religious quarrels tormented Louis XIV until the end of his life but he certainly did not believe that they might imperil the regime itself. Did he perhaps perceive more clearly the results of his foreign policy? We should at least acknowledge the confession that he made on his deathbed at the moment when the Dauphin was presented to him: "I have been too fond of war; do not imitate me in this." Especially after 1672, years of peace were the exception. After the Dutch War that lasted seven years came the War of the League of Augsburg, which lasted ten and then that of the Spanish Succession which continued for almost fourteen. In forty-four years France therefore underwent thirty-one years of war and in the progression from one war to the next the number and determination of her enemies, the extent of the theatres of operation, the number of effectives recruited and maintained, and the expenses necessary to equip, arm, pay and feed them continually increased. Louis XIV doubtless succeeded in retaining within the realm the precious conquests of his minority and youth and assuring her better frontiers by acquiring the Franche-Comté, French Flanders, and Strasbourg which Vauban was able to make practically impregnable. For his successors this was a guarantee of security that benefited the regime. But Louis XIV's subjects did not see this far. Many would doubtless have willingly said, like the author of the *Soupirs de la France esclave*, "The prince's grandeur always brings misery to his subjects." The circumstances that affected them were the material consequences of war: the raising of militia, abuses by the recruiting sergeants, exactions by troops quartered upon the inhabitants, the heavier and more brutally collected *taille*, the tax-gatherer's bailiffs and their seizures, all sorts of taxes invented by the royal tax-farmers, and the misery of famine. After 1672 it was all over for the beautiful order that Colbert, ten years earlier, was so proud of having established in state finances; it was all over for lightening the *taille* and practically balanced budgets. The time had returned for deficits, expedients, and *extraordinary measures* which met unforeseen expenses on a day-to-day basis only with the greatest difficulty. It was once more the triumph of the financiers, so hated by the common people, and the contrast between the crude luxury of the nouveaux riches and the destitution of the beggars and the starving. It was the "court banker," Samuel Bernard, received by the king himself at Versailles and the battles in Paris over the distribution of the "king's bread" at the Louvre.

We know how oppressive was the heritage of financial collapse and popular misery, the two direct consequences of these excessively long wars, that were bequeathed to Louis XIV's successor. We know them well through documents that are certain, numerous, and precise. The financial debacle was so complete that at first it seemed irremediable. It was in vain that new taxes which theoretically were owed by all, the capitation and the twentieth, were added to the traditional levies; the clergy and nobility succeeded in escaping them to a large extent either by paying lump sums or simply not paying them at all. Insufficient receipts led to the deficit that was annually worsened by granting anticipations in the form of advances that consumed the receipts of subsequent years. The floating debt was inordinately increased. In the absence of paper money (since no bank existed to issue it), notes of all sorts circulated: orders to pay creditors, which were veritable treasury bonds, notes from receivers-general which were backed by funds that they levied to advance to the king, promises from the Treasury of Loans created in 1673, and money notes issued against specie that the king ordered melted down before changing its value. All these notes, many of which bore interest, circulated from hand to hand and depreciated each other. A gay time for the speculators whom Dancourt and Lesage portrayed on the stage and singers of satirical songs did not spare. Little did it matter to them! The king could not get along without them for even a week, and so great were the numbers among the bourgeoisie, the nobility, and even the court that had a stake in such matters that they felt themselves invulnerable and every attempt toward fiscal reform seemed all but impossible. From 1715 to the Revolution, financial troubles allowed only brief periods of respite to the monarchy of the old regime which never succeeded in placing its finances on a sound footing.

Evidences of general misery abound and are such that one cannot read them without a feeling of horror. Some are found in the book of Gaiffe, *L'Envers du grand siècle*. The two publications of Arthur de Boislisle, the *Mémoires des intendants sur l'état des généralités*, and the *Correspondance des intendants avec les contrôleurs généraux*, as well as Boisguillebert's *Détail de la France*, are inexhaustible sources of such information. It is not my purpose to describe it here. What must be said is that although certain moments such as the terrible winter of 1709 were doubtless more dreadful than others, general misery never ceased after the middle of the reign. Also it desolated much more than the countryside; even in Paris neither La Reynie nor d'Argenson, in spite of their intelligent efforts, succeeded in ridding the city of beggars and vagabonds. Actually a lengthy peace was capable of redressing the ill effects of war, and misery was no more widespread in France at the end of Louis XIV's reign than it had been a century earlier at the close of the Wars of Religion. But it was momentous that an all-powerful king with nothing to limit his authority was incapable of either avoiding or remedying these calamities; it was momentous that all could see that the pitiful condition of the realm was the natural consequence of his policies. The people's misery facilitated the subjects' alienation and furnished irrefutable arguments to the opposition that was beginning to take shape against the regime. . . .

[There follows a summary of the growth of hostile opinion that developed extensively in France and abroad during the second half of Louis XIV's reign.]

We are familiar with the gloom and mourning in the midst of which the reign and the life of Louis XIV came to an end, isolated in Versailles and shunned by the indifferent and hostile nation. When he died on September 1, 1715, the fate of the monarchy of the old regime was sealed. It survived him another seventy-five years, but its history during the eighteenth century is merely the story of its slow dissolution under the impact of new forces that were building another France and were impossible to reconcile with the regime. The end of absolute monarchy is another subject of study that I shall not undertake.

The monarchy of the old regime was born of the civil wars that ruined France during the second half of the sixteenth century. It accomplished an important work which it is not my purpose to examine here. With Henry IV it pacified the realm and renewed the wellsprings of its prosperity. With Louis XIII and Richelieu it put an end to the dispersal of national energies, disciplined them, and directed them toward a common objective. With Mazarin and Louis XIV it conquered several provinces that were quickly assimilated and gave France solid frontiers. It made our country a very great power, great for a moment because of the strength of her army and greater in a more lasting way because of the prestige of a civilization to which all Europe paid tribute. One of the most brilliant periods of our history parallels that of the monarchy of the old regime.

But although she achieved a work of national significance, she was unable to give her authority a national basis. In this she remained a prisoner of the past. She retained the ancient characteristics of personal monarchy and was unable to develop without emptying of substance the institutions that might have sustained her. She committed the irreparable error of believing that it suffices for a government to be strong. At the end of the seventeenth century, to borrow from Lavisse a metaphor that he borrowed from Lemontey, "the columns on which royalty rested had become hollow." The administrative institutions created by Louis XIV and Colbert provided no remedy; they increased the strength of royal power but did not associate it with the nation. In the presence of a society that was changing, the monarchy of the old regime was isolated and incapable of changing with it. She was doomed.

12   *Charles Godard*
          The Historical Role of the Intendants

Charles Godard was a student of French institutional history dur-
ing the years at the turn of the century. Although the book that is
excerpted here antedates the later special studies of individual in-
tendancies, it retains its value as a work of synthesis. In these pages,
Godard attempts to weigh the contributions and deficiencies of the
intendants in the developed system of institutionalized absolutism
under Louis XIV.

The study of the powers of the intendants is both necessary
and sufficient to portray almost the complete administrative functioning of the monarchy of Louis XIV. . . .

Beginning with Colbert, the intendants' administrative functions
became infinitely varied. New rules of administration were established, required by the necessities of the epoch and having an
essentially modern character.

Colbert determined more precisely than ever before what was
an administrative matter, that is, what concerned the revenues
from the royal rights and the royal domain or the general prosperity of the realm and took from the courts the greater part of
their administrative functions. But the intendants' powers were
never defined with complete precision by their commissions, the
decrees of the royal council, royal ordinances and declarations,
and ministers' letters. . . .

Royal judges above all, the intendants in the time of Richelieu
and Mazarin had contended against other administrators, but
during Colbert's ministry they progressively ceased to struggle
and instead constantly encroached upon almost all other judicial

SOURCE. Charles Godard, *Les Pouvoirs des intendants sous Louis XIV,*
particulièrement dans les pays d'élections, de 1661 à 1715, Paris: Sirey,
1901, pp. 438–445. Translated for this book by William F. Church. Published in 1901 by Librairie Sirey, 22 rue Soufflot, Paris.

and administrative powers. Sometimes their authority merely paralleled another; sometimes it was superposed on the later, while at other times it almost abolished the other altogether even though the king and his ministers more than once restrained their intendants' zeal.

As permanent inspectors-general of all jurisdiction and administration, the intendants shared with the First Presidents of the Parlements the power of surveillance over all judges. Effective direction of the highest police functions became one of their special attributes as well as cognizance of administrative cases and the authority to judge royal officials by virtue of a previous decree from the Council of Dispatches conferring such power. According to the letter of the law, an intendant should not on his own authority substitute his action for that of the regular judges, but whenever the negligence of the royal officials made his intervention necessary he judged a civil or criminal case in virtue of the decree conferring this power.

Only in exceptional cases did the Parlements make use of their ancient right to take measures to prevent local shortages, even in cooperation with the intendants. The latter took from them administrative control of the armies, management of local communities, appeals from local courts, the execution of sentences imposed by royal and ecclesiastical courts, evaluation of the advisability of founding convents, primary schools, high schools, universities and reforming these institutions, the policing of religious dissidents and the newly converted, and general direction of the poor law administration, commerce, agriculture, and industry.

They especially oversaw the promulgation and execution of royal edicts.

The Treasurers of France and the *élus* were reduced to mere intendants' assistants for distributing quarters to the military and assessing the *tailles* and other existing direct taxes, while in the *pays d'élections* the intendants completely controlled such extraordinary levies as the capitation and the tenth.

The competence of the *cours des aides* was sharply diminished. In their places, the intendants collected taxes on offices, audited the cities' debts, income from the royal domain and individuals' revenue from the domain, judged charges for administering the domain and, in the first instance, heard cases between tax-farmers and tax-payers. Authorization to establish a municipal tax was no longer granted by a *cour des aides* but by the controller general on the basis of the intendant's report.

Auditing the accounts of the general collectors of taxes, those who collected the *tailles* and generally all who managed the king's funds was also reserved to the intendants who thereby encroached upon the functions of the Treasurers of France and the *chambres des comptes*.

The Treasurers of France also lost jurisdiction over cases between property owners and contractors for public works, general control over the system of roads and jurisdiction over public projects.

Supervision of the provincial estates remained divided between the governors, the intendants and certain ecclesiastics or presiding officers, but the first two exercised the preponderant roles.

General control over the Catholic clergy was also divided between the bishops and the intendants. Temporary administration of vacant bishoprics, regulation of elections in the abbeys, financial control of parishes, and arbitration between priests and their parishioners came under the intendants' competence. In strange ways, they influenced the elections to the Assembly of the Clergy every five years.

As for the governors who retained supreme command over the troops in the provinces, they were able to exercise this authority only in conjunction with the intendants who were in charge of supplies. The governors and their lieutenants lost as much authority as the Parlements. Moreover, as in matters of royal taxation, every new activity such as recruiting militia, sailors, gunners, and guards for the coasts came under the intendants' control. For financial reasons, general direction of depots, barracks, military hospitals, arsenals, and even fortifications was also reserved to them.

After Louis XIV's death, when the Duke du Maine and Philip V of Spain attempted to combat the Regent, not a single governor would have been able to begin the *Fronde* once more. The preservation of the intendants . . . therefore spared France a new civil war.

In spite of the help given by their subdelegates and the functions that were left to a great many older administrators whom Louis XIV could not dismiss for lack of financial resources with which to repurchase their offices, the intendants were soon too overloaded with functions to handle everything themselves. To increase the number of subdelegates could remedy this situation only by reestablishing in another form the tyranny of local judges who were too often biased and notoriously venal.

Lack of resources, especially after Colbert's death, obliged Louis XIV to increase the number of venal offices. The intendants consequently had many new assistants subordinated to their control: inspectors of the bureaus to collect the *tailles* and payments from the *fermes* (created in 1689), inspectors of factories (created in the same year) having under them the two commissioners for industry established in each Generality, the inspectors-guardians of customs (created in 1708), general and special inspectors of breeding-studs, engineers and their superiors acting as general inspectors, nine treasurers and general keepers of provisions, fodder and depots as well as thirty commissioners for military reviews.

Louis XIV, far from giving up part of his authority, governed more and more in person. The intendants likewise administered and controlled more and more but were able to leave the handling of details to an increasing number of subdelegates and functionaries subject to their control.

Thus modern bureaucracy, beginning in this period, became more and more complicated.

At all times during Louis XIV's long reign, large numbers of decrees of the royal council and even royal ordinances, edicts, regulations, and declarations especially concerning matters of finance, commerce, industry, and religious affairs were inspired and even prepared and drawn up in advance by the intendants. The latter increased the importance of the council which in turn strengthened the intendants' powers by legitimizing their encroachments by means of these regulations.

The intendants' willingness to innovate has often been noted. Foucault took it upon himself to send vagrants to the galleys instead of expelling them. Marillac had the inglorious distinction of inventing the dragonades. Foucault caused the boundaries of the *élections* to be redrawn. D'Aguesseau attempted to make the real *taille* universal. Morant proposed the suppression of internal tolls. And in 1700 Trudaine advised the creation of a Bank of France.

Through the power of centralization, Louis XIV's ministers and intendants assured the realm extraordinary development of national activity, suppression of brigandage and the worst abuses committed by the nobles and justices, the benefits of extraordinary justice without cost, severe control that won French administration its reputation for honesty, regular accounting in the cities and communities, and a notable decline of wrongs and vexations in matters of direct taxation. Indispensable agents of the great creations of Louis XIV and his ministers, the intendants developed the breeding of cattle, commerce, industry, public works, and regularized administration of the poor law and the armies, without, however, preventing abuses on the part of the soldiery.

If the intendants had not been created, the French people whose character and traditions did not embody what was necessary for constant resistance to encroachment would have been abandoned to the capricious despotism of country squires, new nobles who held state offices, and urban oligarchies that were in a fair way to becoming nobility. In the absence of liberty, consistent despotism is preferable. There is always the possibility that administrative tutelage may be skillful and impartial, whereas it is much less likely that a local potentate will have both administrative skill and impartiality.

The faults of the royal government are to be found among its habitual agents. History is correct in blaming the intendants for having abused their power to crush the slightest evidence of independence on the part of the provincial estates, having occasionally allowed themselves to be corrupted like local magistrates, and above all for having done violence to the Protestants' consciences by odious measures. Boulainvilliers said of the intendants, "The earth never sustained more dangerous citizens. These men, absorbed by a frenzy of ambition, readily sacrificed their country to their desire to command as they sacrificed their consciences to court favor. . . . In the midst of calamities, . . . they took care to reveal only those aspects that were unfavorable to the ruler's interests while interrupting the receipt of taxes."

In order to judge the intendants equitably, we should recall that Bezons sought reduction of the taxes that burdened Languedoc, that le Blanc, Bégon, d'Herbigny, and d'Aguesseau were lenient toward the persecuted Protestants, that Ménars opposed seizing the cattle of those who owed taxes, that d'Herbigny, Legendre, and even Foucault and Basville pointed to the raising of the militia as a new factor ruining the peasants, that several in their correspondence showed pity for the misery of the common people, that Basville who proposed the capitation did all possible, as did many others, to ensure that the tax of the tenth did not overwhelm all classes of society, and that ordinarily the intendants attempted to distribute the burden of public taxation according to justice. Boulainvillers does not distinguish the intendants of the last years of the reign, always preoccupied with collecting ruinous levies to meet the expenses of perpetual war, from the zealous administrators of the first period of Louis XIV's personal government. The cruel suffering of the people during the period of increasing misery should be attributed to the king who was more and more isolated at Versailles and almost never spoke to an intendant, much less a peasant as Henry IV had done as well as those who carried out his orders. Saint-Simon gives us a completely erroneous picture of Louis XIV, showing him drowned in detail by ministers who sought to oblige him to give up part of his authority to them. On the contrary, after the death of Colbert and Louvois the king attempted to mould the new ministers, governed from his chambers after the manner of Philip II, and made it known to the intendants and secretaries of state that he controlled them as Colbert had earlier.

We may also reproach Louis XIV for having believed that in the absence of a school of administration, the attendance of the young Masters of Requests[1] in the council of state might provide adequate training for these future viceroys upon whom the fate of the provinces depended, for having assured the intendants' sons, like those of the ministers, reversion of offices that were

---

[1] The *maîtres des requêtes de l'Hôtel du roi* were a large group of trained men, usually lawyers, who were attached to the royal council. From them were drawn most of the intendants and many other officeholders of high rank. (Editor's note.)

often unmerited, and for having made the offices of the subdelegates venal, that is, for having (briefly, it is true) reestablished
the omnipotence of certain local tyrants. The training of the
principal administrators of the state should have been accompanied
by better guarantees, and the harsh judgment of Boulainvillers
regarding the incompetence of far too many administrators certainly contains a modicum of truth.

13   *Charles W. Cole*
                    The Limited Success of Colbert

*Charles W. Cole has enjoyed a highly varied career, first as pro-
fessor of history and economics and later as a high-ranking administrator in various educational and governmental positions. His publications have been chiefly in the field of economic history and theory,
and his works on French mercantilism in the seventeenth century
are held in high esteem. In the present selection, which forms the
conclusion of his most extensive study, Cole attempts the very difficult task of evaluating both the short and long-term contributions of
Colbert to the growth of the French economy. That he finds only
a limited positive contribution during the reign of Louis XIV may
be attributed not so much to Colbert's specific failures as to the
adverse influence of the king's broader policies.*

By any definition of genius, it is hard to apply that word to
Colbert. His was the ability not to originate but to apply. He
thought along old established lines with a dogged tenacity that
argues a certain limitation of vision, as his delight in discovering
and imparting truisms argues even a limitation of his intellectual

SOURCE. Charles W. Cole, *Colbert and a Century of French Mercantilism*,
New York: Columbia University Press, 1939, Vol. II, pp. 549–553, 555, 557–
558. Reprinted by permission of Columbia University Press and the author.
Copyright 1939 by Columbia University Press, New York.

capacity. Where he shone was in his devotion to his king, his country, and his economic preconceptions. Considering the times, he was a great administrator, certainly one of the greatest of his century. If he had any genius, it was a genius for unremitting toil.

Yet it was probably his very limitations that enabled Colbert to succeed so far as he did. A man with more intelligence or vision would have seen both sides of many questions, would have hesitated and temporized, would have bowed before the stubborn inertia of the masses or the opposition of the classes. A man less dogged would have given up in despair or would have become disgusted by a comparison of possible accomplishments with actual achievements. One way of conceiving Colbert's career would be to think of him as an able, energetic, and devoted subordinate, obeying the inherited behests of a long line of French mercantilist thinkers stretching back through Eon and Richelieu to Montchrétien, Laffemas, and Bodin, and of a long line of mercantilist officials, who had for two centuries been drawing up relatively ineffective laws and setting relatively important precedents.

From yet another point of view it might be held that Colbert was inevitable. Given the mercantilist traditions of France, given the great increase and centralization of power that took place under Louis XIV, there was bound to be some administrator, some royal servant who would combine the two tendencies and produce in France an effective effort to put the mercantilist tenets into practice on a nation-wide scale. This thesis might be reënforced by the example of England, where the decay of royal power and of a strong central administration after 1660 gradually impaired the effectiveness of the traditional mercantilism in internal economic life and left only the external (commercial and colonial) mercantilism, which was developed in the late seventeenth and early eighteenth century through the coöperation of Parliament with powerful pressure groups among the bourgeoisie, and paid for by sops to the landholding classes (the corn laws). From still another angle, Colbert's work might be regarded as a vigorous but somewhat premature attempt to modernize French administrative and economic life.

When all is said, however, it must be granted that Colbert represents something more than the heir of a tradition, or a historical necessity. He had, at least, the ability to see France as a unit, and to sum up the varied and disparate elements of French mercantilism into a consistent whole. He had the ability to organize, almost single-handed, a tremendous effort to attain the objectives set up in the preceding century. He had the ability to administer this thousand-faceted movement, in the face of a multitude of obstacles. He had the ability as a courtier to persuade the king of the validity of his plans and the worth of his ends, and to secure the coöperation for more than two decades of a monarch who was not much interested in economic matters. Without Colbert, it is more than likely that something like Colbertism would have come to France after 1661. But it would, perhaps, have been less well organized, less well rounded, less effective than it was.

That Colbert succeeded so well in his superhuman, self-appointed task is the surprising thing. Yet it is worth while to analyze the causes of his failure, which was certainly more than partial, both for his day and for the future. These causes were many and over some of them Colbert had no control. It is probable, for instance, that his plan to rebuild the industrial and commercial life of France was too ambitious, in view of the technology of the century. Given better communications, given a more efficient industrial technique, given a more highly developed business structure, or a more intelligent business class, he might have succeeded better, though it is also quite possible that these very things might have undermined his mercantilist thinking and made his efforts inappropriate. Or again had there been no Hundred Years' War and had the triumph of royal power and the centralization of government come earlier in France, Colbert might have had a more effective administrative machine with which to work. As it was, he had to spend most of his time contending with historically insubordinate elements, and he had the greatest difficulty in securing obedience to his simplest mandates.

But more central in Colbert's failure was a matter that arose from his own thinking and was an integral part of his own program. Whatever aspect of Colbert's labors are studied, it seems that his lack of success or incomplete success was due to the Dutch war. It was this war that impaired his financial reforms and drove him to the *affaires extraordinaires* that he detested. It was this war that ruined the Company of the North, the Insurance Company, the Levant Company, all but ruined the East India Company, and checked the progress of the West Indies. It was this war that shut down the flow of subsidies to industry and commerce and shipbuilding. It was this war that reduced the value of the inspectors of manufactures, by making their remuneration partially dependent on local fees.

Disastrous to his plans as it was, the Dutch war was of necessity approved by Colbert and sprang directly from the very core of his type of mercantilism. If commerce, shipping, industry, and the supply of bullion were all static, as Colbert believed, if one nation could make gain only from the losses of another, then indeed the Dutch were the mortal enemies of France, because of their peculiar and dominant position in the seventeenth century. At them must be aimed taxes and tariffs, companies and industrial subsidies, and such steps were bound to drive the Dutch to a vigorous defense of their supremacy. Colbert welcomed the Dutch war in 1672; he had started it much earlier. To put it succinctly, Colbert's mercantilism needed peace for its progress, but it made war inevitable.

Colbert's belief in a static economy further impaired the success of his policies by making them appropriate to a static economy, when actually the economic life of the world was changing rapidly. It is probable that his industrial regulations, though simple and flexible in his hands, became brakes on the wheel of progress under his more literal-minded successors. It is possible that his attitude on some innovations, as for instance the introduction of half-beaver hats or the use of the frame for woolen stockings, may have retarded progress, though it is reasonably clear that his contributions to new techniques in textile manufacture, mirror-making, dyeing, and so forth, advanced French technology to a great degree. Colbert's support of the guilds did probably serve to perpetuate in France a type of industrial organization that became increasingly unsuitable in the eighteenth century. But if these factors may have served to reduce the permanent value of Colbert's work, they are probably as nothing compared to the basis he laid for the industrial and commercial supremacy of France in the succeeding century.

It is clear that down to 1763, at least, and possibly down to 1789, France led the world in its volume of industrial production, of foreign commerce, and of domestic trade. While this may have been due in part to factors such as the geographical location, the resources, the population, and the government of France, it seems reasonable to suppose that it was also due in good part to the tremendous impetus given French industry and commerce by the work of Colbert. That the supremacy of France was not more marked and more permanent may be attributed to a variety of factors for many of which Colbert was not responsible and some of which he would undoubtedly have disapproved—the revocation of the Edict of Nantes, which gave to all Europe so many of the industrial techniques which Colbert had patiently acquired for France; the continual wars, which absorbed so much of the resources and man power of France and eventually lost her a good part of Colbert's colonial empire; the neglect of sea power, which opened the road for English domination; the hardening of Colbertism as French officialdom, dazzled by the example of Colbert, followed his policies with a somewhat uninspired emulation. It is true that the wars were due, at least in part, to the economic nationalism and colonial and commercial rivalry which Colbert had fostered. His mercantilism bred a counter-mercantilism in many lands. But, on the other hand, it is also true that Colbert's system by its very nature was tied to the efficiency, the power, and the popularity of the French monarchy, and that their decay was bound to impair the effectiveness of his system.

It is not too much, however, to attribute to Colbert's work some permanent effects. They are to be sought not only in specific institutions, created in whole or in part by him, which have endured into the twentieth century—the state tobacco monopoly, the Gobelins, the Saint-Gobain Company, and the like—but also in certain trends and tendencies. The long perpetuation of French supremacy in styles and in luxury goods, the survival of small-scale business, a somewhat greater willingness to protect the consumer than that displayed by other countries, the neo-mercantilism of the nineteenth and twentieth centuries, the economic controls by the state, and the actual state ownership of various enerprises may all be in some degree part of the French heritage from Colbert. . . .

Whatever the basic reasons behind the fact, Colbertism, by fostering industry and commerce, probably aided the growth of capitalism. The commercial companies, the large-scale industrial plants, the subsidies, the tariffs, and the growth of colonial and over-sea trade all tended to improve the capitalistic techniques, to increase the accumulation of capital, to consolidate the position of capitalistic entrepreneurs, and to stimulate the capitalistic spirit. But the support of the guilds, the regulation of industry, the state-owned enterprises, and the continual intervention by the government may to some degree have retarded the growth of capitalism. In so far as he did foster capitalism, Colbert seems to have done it unwittingly, and he might have regarded the large-scale capitalist enterprises of the eighteenth century with some dismay, since he preferred individual to company management where the former was practicable. . . .

Quite possibly the mercantilism of the sixteenth and seventeenth centuries should be regarded as the logical result of three conditions: the rising tide of nationalism, that accompanied the formation of national states in western Europe; the centralization of governmental functions (*étatisme*) that was part of this movement, and the hard-money economy, which was the transitional stage between the barter of the earlier and the credit of the later period, and which was induced or at least accelerated by the influx of precious metals from overseas. . . . It is perhaps the perfect tribute to Colbert that French mercantilism must be considered as more or less embryonic before him and more or less decadent after him, and that for a definition of French mercantilism one can scarce do better than to say:

Mercantilism in France means that group of theories, policies, and practices arising from the traditions of the country and the conditions of the time, and upheld and applied by Jean-Baptiste Colbert during his years in office, 1661–83, in his effort to secure for the nation, and for the king who symbolized it, power, wealth, and prosperity.

14   *Pierre Goubert*
          The Latent Strength in French Society

Pierre Goubert is currently one of the most outstanding members of the large and flourishing group of French economic and social historians who give major attention to demography. Professor Goubert's eminence in the field is indicated by the fact that he is Professor of Modern History at the University of Paris at Nanterre, Director of Studies at the VIe Section de l'Ecole Pratique des Hautes Etudes in Paris, and President of the Société de Démographie historique. In his recent work that is excerpted here, he presents certain new approaches to the problem of estimating the decline of France under Louis XIV. Professor Goubert insists that adequate information is still unavailable in many areas, and he therefore calls his book an interim report pending the appearance of additional studies, some of which are being done under his supervision. Meanwhile, he does not hesitate to hazard some important views concerning the condition of France in 1715 and the various crosscurrents that were operative in her economy and society. Although Professor Goubert's statistics succeed in qualifying the traditional picture of French decline, he implies that France needed more than anything else a period of peace in which the latent strength of her social and economic system might enable her to recover from the effects of Louis XIV's rule.

To save the state from threatened financial collapse, might not the inherent richness of the realm, reinvigorated by the return of peace, slowly bring about the decisive remedy by means of a vigorous economic revival?

Historians have habitually painted such a dismal picture of France in 1715 that one wonders by what miracle the century

SOURCE. Pierre Goubert, *Louis XIV et vingt millions de Français*, Paris: Librairie Arthème Fayard, 1966, pp. 217–222. Translated for this book by William F. Church. Reprinted by permission of Librairie Arthème Fayard and the author. Copyright 1966 by Librairie Arthème Fayard, Paris.

of Louis XV was able to demonstrate all the currently recognized characteristics of undeniable prosperity.

The misery of France at the close of the great reign needs to be closely analyzed, as certain young historians are attempting to do albeit slowly and with considerable difficulty. For the present, it is necessary when focusing on the single year, 1715, to present important correctives to the overly classic picture of desolation.

It is customary to lament the depopulation of the realm following the famines of 1709–1710 and 1713–1714 and various epidemics that were very severe here and there, especially in 1701, and would soon reappear in 1719 and other years in certain provinces. The low demographic level (apparently uniform throughout the nation and perhaps the lowest since the sixteenth century) seems probable. It is permissible, however, to examine the question from other angles.

On the one hand, a drop in population is not necessarily a calamity when a country contains too many mouths for its production and opportunities for work. On the other, the various fatal disasters principally struck children and the aged, groups that were useless because of little or no productivity. Up to a certain point, their disappearance might ease conditions for the survivors. Those who were most notably lacking in the group of active producers (fifteen to fifty years of age) were the youngest and most vigorous who had been born between 1690 and 1700 in relatively small numbers and struck at an early age by famine, smallpox, typhoid fever, purpura, and dysentery. Few in number, they were the more burdened by taxation whose weight had not ceased to increase. However, with the return of peace they did not lack lands and opportunities for work in view of the rapid commercial revival and easier marketing conditions that seemed imminent. Finally, if the number of baptisms and marriages declined during 1715–1720 to a clear minimum more or less everywhere in France, it should be noted that this was not universal, that the following years ushered in a recovery, and that these things affected only certain age groups. Should we also say that the epizootics of 1714, chiefly bovine but truly terrible for humans, must have dealt a majority of the provinces a blow other than a momentary reduction in the burden of the infantile and the senile?

Should we still bemoan the misery that was everywhere in the countryside and among the peasants, not in 1709 but in 1715? After the uncertainties of 1712 and 1713, from Picardy to Provence the harvests were excellent beginning in 1714; the years 1715, 1716, and 1717 were the same. The price of basic foodstuffs fell almost to the low level of 1704–1705 if not 1686. Only the grain merchants might protest for lack of profits, but they were a minority. In Provence, the price of wine remained reasonable without sinking too low; the same was true of olive oil. If heavy taxation had not continued, the year 1715 in the countryside might have been adorned with reasonably gay colors.

In fact, after the return of peace, farmers and sharecroppers were seen to make new efforts to improve the estates, farms, and homesteads that the owners from 1709 to 1711 had often been obliged to cultivate with their own hands or day laborers for lack of solvent takers. Contracts seem to have been concluded at reasonable prices, lessors and lessees once more finding practically normal working conditions. Soon, however, certain brief and significant but illegal phrases would be introduced into these contracts: rents will be paid in "good gold and silver pieces and not in notes . . . regardless of the action of the prince!" The rural population, more aware of monetary phenomena than formerly, protected itself in its own way from the legislative whims of a state on the verge of bankruptcy. But these cautionary measures had not yet appeared at the time when the old king died.

A vigorous maritime expansion seems to us to have marked the end of the seventeenth century and the beginning of the eighteenth, especially during the periods of peace but also, with exceptions, in time of war. The same impression has been gained— and not only at Saint-Malo—by two historians of the new school, fresh from their theses, Pierre Chaunu for the Spanish Atlantic[1] and René Baehrel for lower Provence,[2] who believe that they

[1] P. Chaunu, *Séville et l'Atlantique*, 1504–1650, Paris, 1955–1960, 8 vols.
[2] R. Baehrel, *Une Croissance, la Basse-Provence rurale (fin du XVIe siècle-1789)*, Paris, 1961.

have revealed a speedy revival of rapidly growing maritime activity at the turn of the century. Reexamination of the earlier, excellent research of the Swedish scholar Dahlgren in the archives of our ports sufficiently supports this generalization with examples.[3] In 1712 about ten vessels left for the South Seas, fifteen in 1713, and twenty in 1714. The *Grand-Dauphin* of Saint-Malo which circled the globe during the height of the war did so again from 1714 to 1717. In a single year, 1714, about twenty French ships traded in the ports of Peru and Chile; others crossed the Pacific to trade with China. In spite of the risks, this commerce was most profitable to the economy of the realm not only because of its return in silver pieces but also its various exports, especially textiles.

Other commercial relations rapidly recovered. Historians of Marseilles similarly show that their great port, on becoming "free" once more, strengthened its influence in the Levant. If the government somewhat neglected the colonial sphere (although less than has been claimed), it nevertheless allowed François Martin to pursue his skillful policy in India and the Senegal Company to penetrate the interior of that country, and granted Antoine Crozat in 1712 the privilege of trading with immense, promising Louisiana. The great western ports, especially Nantes, were already profiting from their ties with the Antilles, particularly Santo Domingo, and established sugar refineries here and there, especially along the Loire. More and more, merchants, officials, townsmen, and even great lords dared invest their funds in maritime enterprises, took "shares" in distant voyages, and acquired "settlements" in Santo Domingo and the Caribbean Isles. A whole aspect of the eighteenth century, certainly not new in 1715, henceforth assumes major importance in the period of newly recovered peace and relative security that the new commercial treaties ensured.

The low price of food, accelerated revival of foreign trade, peace, perhaps a certain inflation, all of these were factors that might have given rise to a renaissance in industry that the traditional historians readily describe as horribly decadent. In this

[3] E. W. Dahlgren, *Les Relations commerciales et maritimes entre la France et les côtes de l'océan pacifique (commencement du XVIIIᵉ siècle)*, Paris, 1909.

area and at this date, 1715, studies in depth are too lacking to permit presenting anything more than an impression. The factories in Picardy that produced woolens for the troops and the Spanish seem to have maintained their production, no more; the new vigor of Amiens and Beauvais began only in the years 1725–1730. As for textiles, we possess no acceptable statistical data. What was left of Colbert's great establishments—the Gobelins and Beauvais, for example—were about to flourish again after experiencing very difficult moments. Metallurgy does not seem strong, especially by comparison, but more and more interest was given coal—a good century after the British. Factories using materials from the colonies were more active.

A moment's hesitation, the requirements of reconversion, difficulties due to monetary problems and the redistribution of international markets, decline here and good starts there, but most often stagnation: such are the impressions left by the weaknesses of available scholarly works. Certainly not an atmosphere of ruin; rather a great waiting. . . .

Have we excessively brightened the dark classic picture of the last year of the reign? Most certainly the dukes and the jurists of the Parlement were preparing to take or regain the power of which they had been forceably deprived. The clergy and all cultivated persons were troubled by the great quarrel of the Gallicans and Jansenists. The Protestant Churches were being reestablished victoriously and illegally in the south and even in Paris. The financial and monetary situation, much more serious than in 1661, seemed without solution, at least by ordinary means. The ranks of the common people, who had suffered so much, were thinner and much misery was to be observed in the countryside and the cities, perhaps more than in 1661. Discharged soldiers, vagabonds, and brigands still infested the thickets and roads of the realm. Almost no technical progress was apparent in the fields and the workshops except in the manufacture of stockings and a few small machines for glossing and pressing cloth. Certainly the maritime and colonial "vocation" of the realm was rather neglected by the state, and the latter now gave hardly any financial support to the artists whom it had attracted earlier. . . .

Nevertheless, except for the ruined Cévennes and certain price riots that were quickly appeased, chronic revolt no longer menaced this or that part of the realm. The soldiers, more and more quartered in barracks, no longer caused fear at the mere mention of their coming; it may be said that this "evil that spread terror" had been conquered and would be contained by 1720. If the king's squadrons no longer dominated the seas, French shipowners and traders maintained numerous substantial and respected ships in the Mediterranean and the oceans. Although the royal administration was currently being criticized, badly obeyed, and menaced, one that was more competent and better armed would slowly be established in the realm. One province, the Franch-Comté, several areas in the north, and a great urban port of entry, Strasbourg, partially reinforced the frontiers that had been strongly secured by Vauban. The prestige of the French language, letters, and arts had been disseminated for a long time to come throughout the cultivated world. Even the financial debacle would be solved within ten years. And most important, seventeen or eighteen million Frenchmen in the fields and the factories were working peacefully and slowly with archaic techniques under precarious conditions but with undeniable courage, skill, ingenuity and perseverance. In the end, it was with them that rested the future and strength of this nation, which was beginning to seek out and find itself on the morrow of the disappearance of the potentate who had been weary, outmoded, and finally detested but who at least left a magnificent image of the religion of royalty of which he had made himself the high priest.

CONCLUSION

All schools of political thought are agreed that the ultimate purpose of government is the benefit of the governed. The exact definition of what is beneficial, however, varies substantially from age to age and is strongly influenced by a host of relevant factors such as conditions of life, the political maturity of the people, the prevailing concept of human nature, and the values associated with life in organized society. The predominant view of such matters in France during the seventeenth century was that which is generally associated with French culture during its classic age. A high premium was placed upon discipline and control in an ordered society that was structured in hierarchical fashion. The various social classes, professional bodies, and other groups should remain in their respective stations within the corporate social organism and be content to make their contributions to the whole. Even the higher phases of life such as art, letters, and religion should be ordered so as to approximate a lofty and fixed ideal. Within this context, the role of absolute monarchy was crucial and clear: to discipline the nation and lead it to a higher way of life and great achievements. This meant controls, coercion, even exploitation at home and feats of arms abroad, all of which reached their acme under Louis XIV. The degree of success that the French kings and their ministers achieved during the Age of Absolutism has been adequately indicated above. Through a massive and many-sided program of state-building, they succeeded in increasing royal power, directed the energies of the nation into newly significant channels, met the foreign challenge, and contributed extensively to the growth of the French nation.

Absolutism, however, was far from universally accepted, especially in its practical applications. Opposition from various segments of French society was continual throughout the century. Although the sources and forms of this opposition varied from one generation to the next according to such factors as the burden of royal taxation, the strength of the regime, the means used to control the populace, and the extent of foreign war, major segments of the population invariably found the burdens of absolutism unbearable and resisted with the limited means at their disposal. The fact that opposition was chronic among the governed, that is, those who experienced the actual workings of absolutism and who were ostensibly its ultimate beneficiaries, is crucial in evaluating its significance in the period. Furthermore, absolutism was opposed not only because it involved regimentation and exploitation; to many observers its policies seemed unjust and immoral as several of our selections demonstrate. Violation of traditional rights and the undertaking of questionable wars, they felt, could not be justified by the newly developed ethic of reason of state. To many contemporaries in all walks of life, the price that France was required to pay for her achievements and greatness was excessive.

Opposition during the first half of the century chiefly took the form of peasant uprisings, noble rebellions, and even resistance by the Parlement of Paris. After the failure of the *Fronde,* the nobles and jurists ceased their agitation; acceptance of strong monarchy was general among the upper classes, and the stage was set for the most brilliant moment in the history of French absolutism, the first generation of the reign of Louis XIV. Even during this period, however, peasant revolts continued in many provinces. They were eventually brought under control by a variety of measures, chiefly those instituted by the intendants. But no sooner was this type of opposition mastered than another reappeared in the latter part of the reign, that of the intellectuals. Never entirely absent earlier, it rapidly gained momentum as the reign of the Grand Monarch waned and the cost of his policies became terrible indeed. In addition to the authors excerpted here, the movement included such key writers as Vauban and Boisguillebert in economics, Saint-Simon and Boulainvilliers as spokesmen for the nobility, Massillon among the clergy, the philosopher Bayle, and many others both at home and abroad. Long before Louis XIV's death, the desertion of the intellectuals had reached formidable proportions with dire consequences for the future of absolutism. It should be noted that none of these writers advocated the abolition of absolute monarchy in which the king held all governmental authority; rather, it was Louis XIV's implementation of absolutism, that is, his policies, that they rejected. We now know, however, that these critics of the regime were laying the foundations of the Enlightenment which would ultimately become a major force making for the destruction of the monarchy itself. Because thinking men increasingly rejected Louis XIV's policies while his rule was in full vigor and initiated a movement of criticism that would relentlessly expand after his death, one may conclude that the French people had tried absolutism and found it wanting.

SUGGESTIONS FOR FURTHER READING

These suggested readings are not intended to cover all phases of French history during the seventeenth century but only those that are pertinent to this study, essentially absolutism in action. For printed sources, the indispensible instrument is E. Bourgeois and L. André, *Les Sources de l'histoire de France: XVIIe siècle*, 8 vols., Paris, 1913–1935. For modern works, the most comprehensive listing is E. Préclin and V. L. Tapié, *Le XVIIe siècle ("Clio"): 1610–1715*, Paris, 1949. Recently, the following manual has added further bibliographical information, especially in social and economic history. R. Mandrou, *La France aux XVIIe et XVIIIe siècles ("Nouvelle Clio")*, Paris, 1967. Valuable general bibliographies are contained in the latest editions of the volumes of the Langer Series. C. J. Friedrich, *The Age of the Baroque, 1610–1660*, New York, 1952. F. L. Nussbaum, *The Triumph of Science and Reason, 1660–1685*, New York, 1953. J. B. Wolf, *The Emergence of the Great Powers, 1685–1715*, New York, 1951. Comprehensive listings are to be found in the following bibliographical articles. W. F. Church, "Publications on Cardinal Richelieu since 1945: A Bibliographical Study," *Journal of Modern History*, XXXVII (1965), pp. 421–444. J. B. Wolf, "The Reign of Louis XIV: A Selected Bibliography of Writings Since the War of 1914–1918," *Journal of Modern History*, XXXVI (1964), pp. 127–144.

The following general works contain valuable perspectives on the nature and significance of absolutism in the seventeenth century. E. Lavisse, *Histoire de France*, Vols. 6²–8¹, Paris, 1905, 1911. J. Boulenger, *The Seventeenth Century* (English translation), New York, 1920. R. Mousnier, *Les XVIe et XVIIe siècles*, Paris, 1954. G. Pagès, *La Monarchie d'ancien régime (De Henri*

IV à Louis XIV), Paris, 1932. D. Ogg, *Europe in the Seventeenth Century*, London, 1949. The fifth volume of the *New Cambridge Modern History*, Cambridge, 1961, contains a number of valuable studies. The manuals in the *Que sais-je?* series summarize recent views on many subjects. H. Méthivier, *Le Siècle de Louis XIII*, Paris, 1964, and *Le Siècle de Louis XIV*, Paris, 1962.

On Cardinal Richelieu, by far the best general study is V. L. Tapié, *La France de Louis XIII et de Richelieu*, second edition, Paris, 1967 (with good bibliographies). G. Hanotaux and Duc de La Force, *Histoire du Cardinal de Richelieu*, 6 vols., Paris, 1896–1947, may be consulted on all aspects of the Cardinal's policies. Miss C. V. Wedgwood, *Richelieu and the French Monarchy*, revised edition, New York, 1962, is a good summary of accepted information. For the operation of Richelieu's "rule," the student should begin with G. d'Avenel, *Richelieu et la monarchie absolue*, 4 vols., Paris, 1895. A very important analysis of the rivalry between Richelieu and the *dévot* party is contained in G. Pagès, "Autour du 'Grand Orage': Richelieu et Marillac, deux politiques," *Revue historique*, CLXXIX (1937), pp. 63–97. For Richelieu's political ideas, the best source is his *Testament politique*, L. André, ed., Paris, 1947. Portions are available in English translation in H. B. Hill, ed. and trans., *The Political Testament of Cardinal Richelieu: The Significant Chapters and Supporting Selections*, Madison, 1961. Interesting studies of Cardinal Mazarin are to be found in G. Mongrédien, ed., *Mazarin*, Paris, 1959.

In addition to those of Lavisse, Pagès and Mousnier cited above, the following are among the better general works on Louis XIV. P.-E. Lemontey, *Essai sur l'établissement monarchique de Louis XIV*, Paris, 1818, is quite old but retains considerable value for its interpretations of the reign. One of the better modern works is P. Gaxotte, *La France de Louis XIV*, Paris, 1946. D. Ogg, *Louis XIV*, London, 1933, and M. Ashley, *Louis XIV and the Greatness of France*, London, 1946 (both reprinted in paperbound editions) are able summary treatments. While P. Goubert, *Louis XIV et vingt millions de Français*, Paris, 1966, emphasizes recent developments in economic and social history, it is also a significant general work on the period. The most comprehen-

sive recent study is J. B. Wolf, *Louis XIV*, New York, 1968.
For Louis XIV's concept of monarchy, the fundamental source
is his *Mémoires*, C. Dreyss, ed., 2 vols., Paris, 1860. J. Longnon,
. . . *Mémoires pour les années 1661 et 1666*, Paris, 1923, is a small
portion of the work, published as an uncritical edition. It was
translated by Herbert Wilson and published under the title, *A
King's Lessons in Statecraft, Louis XIV*, London, 1924. Later,
Longnon published a fuller version, *Mémoires de Louis XIV*,
Paris, 1933.

For the concept of absolutism as it was understood in the
seventeenth century, by far the best work is G. Lacour-Gayet,
L'Education politique de Louis XIV. The first edition (Paris,
1898) is preferable because it contains extensive bibliographical
references. In the second (Paris, 1923), the text is revised but
the citations are lacking. H. Sée, *Les Idées politiques en France
au XVIIe siècle*, Paris, 1920, and J. Touchard, *Histoire des idées
politiques*, Vol. I, Paris, 1959, contain convenient introductions
to the subject. Valuable observations concerning absolutism are
contained in R. Mousnier and F. Hartung, "Quelques problèmes
concernant la monarchie absolue," *Relazioni del X Congresso
Internazionale di Scienze Storiche*, Vol. IV, Florence, 1955, pp.
1–55. Major contemporary sources are Richelieu's *Testament
politique*, Louis XIV's *Mémoires* (both cited above) and the
relevant works of Bossuet. The latter are conveniently available
in J. Le Brun, ed., *J.-B. Bossuet, Politique tirée des propres
paroles de l'Ecriture Sainte*, Geneva, 1967, and J. Truchet, ed.,
Politique de Bossuet, Paris, 1966.

The growth of governmental institutions under absolutism has
been treated in many works. In addition to the book by Pagès,
cited above, the following are valuable general studies. G. Pagès,
"L'Evolution des institutions administratives en France du commencement du XVIe siècle à la fin du XVIIe," *Revue d'histoire
moderne*, VII (1932), pp. 8–57. F. Dumont, "Royauté française
et monarchie absolue au XVIIe siècle," *XVIIe siècle*, nos. 58–59
(1963), pp. 3–29. R. Mousnier has contributed the following very
valuable analyses of institutional developments. *La Venalité des
offices sous Henri IV et Louis XIII*, Rouen, 1945. "Le Conseil
du roi de la mort de Henri IV au gouvernement personnel de
Louis XIV," *Etudes d'histoire moderne et contemporaine*, I

(1947), pp. 29–67. "L'Evolution des institutions monarchiques en France et ses relations avec l'état social," *XVIIe siècle*, nos. 58–59 (1963), pp. 57–72. The best recent work on the functioning of the upper reaches of the governmental system under Richelieu is O. A. Ranum, *Richelieu and the Councillors of Louis XIII*, Oxford, 1963. J. E. King attempts to show the "rationalization" of the royal administration under Louis XIV in his *Science and Rationalism in the Government of Louis XIV, 1661–1683*, Baltimore, 1949. E. Glasson, *Le Parlement de Paris, son rôle politique*, Vol. I, Paris, 1901, traces the pressures that the royal government exerted on the Parlement. On the all-important intendants, the following are valuable. R. Mousnier, "Etat et commissaire: Recherches sur la création des intendants des provinces (1634–1648)," in *Forschungen zu Staat und Verfassung: Festgabe für Fritz Hartung*, R. Dietrich, ed., Berlin, 1958, pp. 325–344. C. Godard, *Les Pouvoirs des intendants sous Louis XIV, particulièrement dans les pays d'élections, de 1661 à 1715*, Paris, 1901. G. Livet, *L'Intendance d'Alsace sous Louis XIV, 1648–1715*, Paris, 1956. H. Fréville, *L'Intendance de Bretagne (1689–1790)*, 3 vols., Rennes, 1953. E. Esmonin, *Etudes sur la France des XVIIe et XVIIIe siècles*, Paris, 1964, contains many able studies of the intendants. The strength and effectiveness of Louis XIV's new police system in Paris is well treated in J. Saint-Germain, *La Reynie et la police au grand siècle*, Paris, 1962. The manner in which the intendants forcibly recruited soldiers for Louis XIV's armies during the War of the Spanish Succession is well described in G. A. M. Girard, *Le Service militaire en France à la fin du règne de Louis XIV: racolage et milice (1701–1715)*, Paris, 1921. Interesting details concerning the arbitrary manner in which trials were conducted in this period are available in J. Imbert, ed., *Quelques procès criminels des XVIIe et XVIIIe siècles*, Paris, 1964. P. de Vaissière, *Un Grand Procès sous Richelieu: L'Affaire du Maréchal de Marillac (1630–1632)*, Paris, 1924, and *La Conjuration de Cinq-Mars*, Paris, 1928.

The economic and financial aspects of absolutism have been analyzed in a number of studies. Mercantilism, the economics of state-building, is examined in the following. The standard work is H. Sée, *Histoire économique de la France*, Vol. I, Paris, 1939. J. U. Nef, *Industry and Government in France and England,*

1540–1640, Philadelphia, 1940, is an interesting but limited comparative study. The best treatment of Cardinal Richelieu's economic activities is H. Hauser, *La Pensée et l'action économiques du Cardinal de Richelieu,* Paris, 1944. See also L. A. Boiteux, *Richelieu grand maître de la navigation et du commerce de France,* Paris, 1955, and F. C. Palm, *The Economic Policies of Richelieu,* Urbana, 1922. The various elements of Colbert's massive effort to strengthen the state economically are examined in C. W. Cole, *Colbert and a Century of French Mercantilism,* 2 vols., New York, 1939. His *French Mercantilism, 1683–1700,* New York, 1943, is also valuable. P. Boisonnade, *Colbert, le triomphe de l'étatisme,* Paris, 1932, gives a somewhat different picture of Colbert and attributes greater success to his efforts than does Cole. G. Mongrédien, *Colbert,* Paris, 1963, is a recent general work. R. Mousnier, "L'Evolution des finances publiques en France et en Angleterre pendant les guerres de la ligue d'Augsbourg et de succession d'Espagne," *Revue historique,* CCV (1951), pp. 1–23, is a good analysis of the workings of public finance. J. Saint-Germain, *Samuel Bernard, le banquier des rois,* gives an interesting picture of a famous financier. The studies on royal taxation are unfortunately fragmentary and the subject must be investigated in such works as the following. J. J. Clamageran, *Histoire de l'impôt en France,* 3 vols., Paris, 1867–1876, is quite old but still useful. The best special study is E. Esmonin, *La Taille en Normandie au temps de Colbert (1661–1683),* Paris, 1913. J. Meuvret, "Comment les français du XVIIᵉ siècle voyaient l'impôt," *XVIIᵉ siècle,* nos. 25–26 (1955), pp. 59–82, examines contemporary attitudes toward royal taxation.

The materials on the social history of France during the period are many and varied. The two publications edited by A. M. de Boislisle, *Mémoires des intendants sur l'état des généralités dressés pour l'instruction du duc de Bourgogne,* Paris, 1881, and *Correspondence des contrôleurs généraux des finances avec les intendants des provinces,* 3 vols., Paris, 1874–1897, are fundamental sources. The best general modern work is P. Sagnac, *La Formation de la société française moderne,* Vol. I, Paris, 1945. Various elements of social history may be gleaned from D. Ogg, *Europe in the Seventeenth Century,* London, 1949; G. N. Clark, *The Seventeenth Century,* Oxford, 1947; and J. Lough, *An Introduc-*

tion to Seventeenth Century France, London, 1954. Intimate views of the conditions of life are found in F. A. Gaiffe, *L'Envers du grand siècle*, Paris, 1924, E. Magne, *La Vie quotidienne au temps de Louis XIII*, Paris, 1947, G. Mongrédien, *La Vie quotidienne sous Louis XIV*, Paris, 1948, and J. Saint-Germain, *La Vie quotidienne en France à la fin du grand siècle*, Paris, 1965. The following are valuable studies of the French nobility. G. d'Avenel, *La Noblesse française sous Richelieu*, Paris, 1901 (reprinted from Vols. I and II of his *Richelieu et la monarchie absolue*, Paris, 1895). P. de Vaissière, *Gentilshommes campagnards de l'ancienne France*, Paris, 1925. E. Teall, "The Seigneur of Renaissance France," *Journal of Modern History*, XXXVII (1965), pp. 131–150. O. A. Ranum, "Richelieu and the Great Nobility: Some Aspects of Early Modern Political Motives," *French Historical Studies*, III (1963), pp. 184–204. R. B. Grassby, "Social Status and Commercial Enterprise under Louis XIV," *Economic History Review*, XIII (1960), pp. 19–38.

The evolution of French society under absolute monarchy may be partially measured by examining the following regional studies. G. Roupnel, *La Ville et la campagne au XVIIᵉ siècle: Etude sur les populations du pays dijonnais*, Paris, 1955 (first published in 1922). P. Goubert, *Beauvais et le Beauvaisis de 1600 à 1730: Contribution à l'histoire sociale de la France du XVIIᵉ siècle*, 2 vols., Paris, 1960. R. Baehrel, *Une Croissance: La Basse-Provence rurale, 1590–1789*, Paris, 1961. E. Le Roy Ladurie, *Les Paysans du Languedoc*, 2 vols., Paris, 1966. P. Deyon, *Amiens capitale provinciale: Etude sur la société urbaine au XVIIᵉ siècle*, Paris, 1967. To these should be added the following significant articles. R. Mousnier, "Etudes sur la population de la France au XVIIᵉ siècle," *XVIIᵉ siècle*, no. 16 (1952), pp. 527–542. J. Meuvret, "Les Crises de subsistances et la démographie de la France d'ancien régime," *Population*, I (1946), pp. 643–650. R. Baehrel, "Statistique et démographie historique: la mortalité sous l'ancien régime, remarques inquiètes," *Annales: économies, sociétés, civilisations*, XII (1957), pp. 85–98.

Scholars have recently emphasized the inherent tensions and frictions in European society that made for a continual crisis in social relations. Professor Mousnier, in his *Les XVIᵉ et XVIIᵉ siècles*, Paris, 1954, extensively supports this interpretation. For related materials and views, the following may be consulted. E. Hobsbawm, "The General Crisis of the European Economy in the Seventeenth Century," *Past and Present*, 1954, No. 5, pp. 33–53; No. 6, pp. 44–65. H. R. Trevor-Roper, "The General Crisis of the Seventeenth Century," *Past and Present*, 1959, No. 16, pp. 31–64. Discussion of Trevor-Roper's article by E. H. Kossmann, E. J. Hobsbawm, J. H. Hexter, R. Mousnier, J. H. Elliott, L. Stone, and H. R. Trevor-Roper in *Past and Present*, 1960, No. 18, pp. 8–42. These articles are reproduced in part, and with additions, in T. Aston, ed., *Crisis in Europe, 1560–1660*, London, 1965.

Popular uprisings have received major attention from scholars in recent years. B. Porchnev, *Les Soulèvements populaires en France de 1623 à 1648*, Paris, 1963 (French translation), is the fundamental general work, characterized by extensive research and strong Marxist bias. A more traditional interpretation is presented in R. Mousnier, "Recherches sur les soulèvements populaires en France avant la Fronde," *Revue d'histoire moderne et contemporaine*, V (1958), pp. 81–113. See also Mousnier's valuable synthesis, *Fureurs paysannes: Les Paysans dans les révoltes du XVIIe siècle*, Paris, 1967, Part I and Conclusion. Further views may be found in R. Mandrou, "Les Soulèvements populaires et la société française du XVIIe siècle," *Annales: économies, sociétés, civilisations*, XIV (1959), pp. 756–765, and *Classes et luttes de classes en France au début du XVIIe siècle*, Florence, 1965. The following articles are also valuable relative to this important phenomenon. P. Deyon, "A propos des rapports entre la noblesse française et la monarchie absolue pendant la première moitié du XVIIe siècle," *Revue historique*, CCXXXI (1964), pp. 341–356. L. Bernard, "French Society and Popular Uprisings under Louis XIV," *French Historical Studies*, III (1963–64), pp. 454–474. An excellent summary of the many ramifications of the Porchnev-Mousnier controversy, with indications concerning possible further research, is J. H. M. Salmon, "Venality of Office and Popular Sedition in Seventeenth Century France," *Past and Present*, 1967, No. 37, pp. 21–43. The best body of source material in this area is R. Mousnier, ed., *Lettres et mémoires adressées au Chancelier Séguier (1633–1649)*, 2 vols., Paris, 1964. G. Walter, *Histoire des paysans de France*, Paris, 1963, contains good accounts of the major popular uprisings and has extensive bibliographies.

The *Fronde*, which was the most extensive and important rebellion against increasing absolutism, is treated in the following works. E. H. Kossmann, *La Fronde*, Leiden, 1954, is the best general book on the subject. P. Doolin, *The Fronde*, Cambridge, Mass., 1935, is much more limited, stressing institutional and legal matters. Interesting aspects of the uprising are treated in L. Madelin, *La Fronde*, Paris, 1931, and P. G. Lorris, *La Fronde*, Paris, 1961. The following are valuable special studies. R. Mousnier, "Quelques raisons de la Fronde: les causes des journées révolutionnaires parisiennes de 1648," *XVIIe siècle*, No. 2–3 (1949), pp. 33–78. J. Jacquart, "La Fronde des princes dans la région parisienne et ses conséquences matérielles," *Revue d'histoire moderne et contemporaine*, VII (1960), pp. 257–290.

The religious policies of the royal government have been examined by a number of very able scholars. The relations between the monarchy and the Roman Catholic Church may be examined in the following standard works. A. Fliche and V. Martin, eds., *Histoire de l'église depuis les origines jusqu'à nos jours*, Vols. XVIII, XIX, Paris, 1955, 1960 (with bibliographies), and G. Goyau, *Histoire religieuse de la France*, Paris, 1922. The institutional relationships between the crown and the French Church are carefully analyzed in P. Blet, *Le Clergé de France et la monarchie: Etude sur les assemblées générales du clergé de 1615 à 1666*, 2 vols., Rome, 1959. The best work on seventeenth-century Gallicanism is A. G. Martimort, *Le Gallicanisme de Bossuet*, Paris, 1953. For royal policy relative to the Jansenists, the following standard works are of value. C. A. Sainte-Beuve, *Port-Royal*, 7 vols., Paris, 1927 (various eds.) and A. Gazier, *Histoire générale du mouvement janséniste*, Vol. I, Paris, 1923. For Richelieu and the Jansenists, the fundamental work is J. Orcibal, *Les Origines du jansénisme*, Vol. II, Paris, 1947. Orcibal expertly summarizes his findings concerning Richelieu's persecution of Saint-Cyran in his *Saint-Cyran et le jansénisme*, Paris, 1961. J. Orcibal, *Louis XIV contre Innocent XI*, Paris, 1949, examines the king's relations with the papacy during a particularly difficult period. A general treatment of royal policy may be found in

W. J. Stankiewicz, *Politics and Religion in Seventeenth Century France*, Berkeley, 1960.

The best general analysis of royal policy toward the French Huguenots is in E. G. Léonard, *Histoire générale du protestantisme*, Vol. II, Paris, 1961 (with bibliographies). See also his "Le Protestantisme français au XVIIe siècle," *Revue historique*, CC (1948), pp. 153–179. The best modern work on Louis XIV and the Revocation of the Edict of Nantes is J. Orcibal, *Louis XIV et les protestants*, Paris, 1951. See also D. Robert, "Louis XIV et les protestants," *XVIIe siècle*, Nos. 76–77 (1967), pp. 39–52. H. M. Baird, *The Huguenots and the Revocation of the Edict of Nantes*, 2 vols., New York, 1895, contains much information but is strongly biased in favor of the persecuted. Louis XIV's failure to extirpate Calvinism is shown in A. Ducasse, *La Guerre des camisards: La Resistance huguenote sous Louis XIV*, Paris, 1962. W. C. Scoville, *The Persecution of the Huguenots and French Economic Development, 1680–1720*, Berkeley, 1960, expertly shows that the economic impact of the Revocation was not as great as formerly believed.

Among the many treatments of French foreign policy, the following are sufficient to indicate the causes and nature of the many wars in which France was involved. G. Zeller, *Les Temps modernes (Histoire des relations internationales*, Vols. II, III), Paris, 1953, 1955, summarizes the essentials. On the Thirty Years' War, C. V. Wedgwood, *The Thirty Years' War*, London, 1938, is an able, thorough treatment. G. Pagès, *La Guerre de trente ans*, Paris, 1939, is a good standard work, and G. Livet, *La Guerre de trente ans*, Paris, 1963, expertly summarizes recent contributions to knowledge of the war and its impact upon Europe. Aldous Huxley, in his *Grey Eminence*, New York, 1941, uses the career of Father Joseph to present a very interesting thesis concerning the futility of using war to serve higher causes. For Louis XIV's foreign policy, the best general work is L. André, *Louis XIV et l'Europe*, Paris, 1950. See also André's *Michel le Tellier et Louvois*, Paris, 1942, which is a valuable study of the dynamics of war and Louvois' role in influencing royal policy. G. Zeller definitely lays to rest the legend that the French rulers in the seventeenth century sought to extend the boundaries of France to her "natural" frontiers in "La Monarchie d'ancien régime et les frontières naturelles," *Revue d'histoire moderne*, VIII (1933), pp. 305-333, and "Histoire d'une idée fausse," *Revue de synthèse*, LVI (1936). The latter is reprinted in G. Zeller, *Aspects de la politique française sous l'ancien régime*, Paris, 1964. Important elements of Louis XIV's foreign policy are analyzed by ranking experts in "Problèmes de politique étrangère sous Louis XIV," *XVIIe siècle*, Nos. 46-47 (1960).

The growth of opposition to Louis XIV's policies during the second half of the reign is clearly evident in the following. The more important primary sources are the relevant works of Fénelon, Saint-Simon, Bayle, Jurieu, Vauban, Boisguillebert, Boulainvillers, and the funeral oration for Louis XIV that the famous preacher Jean Baptiste Massillon gave in the Sainte-Chapelle. Among modern works, P. Hazard, *The European Mind: The Critical Years, 1680-1715*, New Haven, 1953 (English translation) is the standard treatment of the changed mentality that provided the groundwork for increasing criticism. The best treatment of the growth of hostile opinion in Germany is H. Gillot, *Le Règne de Louis XIV et l'opinion publique en Allemagne*, Nancy, 1914. Increasing criticism of mercantilism, theoretical and practical, is traced in the following. H. V. Roberts, *Boisguillebert, Economist of the Reign of Louis XIV*, New York, 1935, and parts of C. W. Cole, *French Mercantilism, 1683-1700*, New York, 1943. A major source is Vauban, *Projet d'une dixme royale*, F. Coornaert, ed., Paris, 1933. L. Rothkrug, *Opposition to Louis XIV: The Political and Social Origins of the French Enlightenment*, Princeton, 1965, extensively treats the theoretical elements of growing antimercantilism. The career and writings of Boulainvillers are thoroughly examined in R. Simon, *Henry de Boulainviller*, Paris, 1941, and *Un Revolté du grand siècle, Henry de Boulainviller*, Paris, 1948. Among the many works on Pierre Bayle and growing rationalism, the following are of major importance. E. Labrousse, *Pierre Bayle*, 2 vols., The Hague, 1963, 1964. H. Robinson, *Bayle the Skeptic*, New York, 1931. W. Rex, *Essays on Pierre Bayle and Religious Controversy*, The Hague, 1965. The writings of the Huguenots in exile against Louis XIV are extensively examined in G. H. Dodge, *The Political Theory of the Huguenots of the Dispersion, with Special Reference to the Thought and Influence of Pierre Jurieu,* New York, 1947. Although Fénelon's political ideas were but a minor part of his thought, they have received considerable attention. *Fénelon: Ecrits et lettres politiques,* C. Urbain, ed., Paris, 1920, is the most convenient edition of his political tracts. The most extensive recent treatment of a key portion of Fénelon's career is R. Schmittlein, *L'Aspect politique du differend Bossuet-Fénelon,* Baden, 1954 (with bibliographies). F. Gallouédec-Genuys, *Le Prince selon Fénelon,* Paris, 1963, brings together the essentials. For Fénelon's relations with the Duke of Burgundy and plans for reform, see G. Tréca, *Les Doctrines et les réformes de droit public en réaction contre l'absolutisme de Louis XIV dans l'entourage du duc de Bourgogne,* Paris, 1909. Valuable articles on Fénelon are contained in a special issue of *XVIIᵉ siècle,* Nos. 12-14 (1952).

ADDENDUM. The following forthcoming volumes contain materials that bear directly upon seventeenth century absolutism. O. A. Ranum, *Paris in the Seventeenth Century,* New York, 1968. J. C. Rule, ed., *Louis XIV and the Craft of Kingship,* Columbus, 1969.

LIST OF UNTRANSLATED
FRENCH TERMS

Because many French administrative and financial terms lack exact English equivalents, any effort to translate them in the above selections might be very misleading. They have therefore been left untranslated and the following meanings supplied.

Aides. Indirect taxes; excises on a large variety of articles and transactions. Resisted and criticized because of their arbitrary nature and uneven application throughout the realm.

Apanage. Land held for his support by a member of the royal family other than the king.

Bailliage. Territorial unit over which the bailli, an agent of the crown, exercised administrative and especially judicial power.

Chambre des comptes. Sovereign court for the examination of the administration of royal finances and the preservation of the royal domain. Combined administrative and judicial powers. The most important such court was in Paris; others were in the provinces.

Cours des aides. Courts that were established throughout France for the administration of the *aides* and jurisdiction over cases concerning these and other taxes.

Ecu. French coin. The most common type was of silver and was valued at three *livres* or sixty *sous*.

Elections, élus. Royally appointed tax-collectors in the provinces that lacked provincial estates were called *élus* because they were originally elected locally. This practice had completely disappeared before the seventeenth century and they were mere royal agents, usually working under the direction of the intendants. The areas in which they functioned were called *élections*.

Ferme, fermier. A large number of indirect taxes including the salt tax, *aides,* tolls, etc., were farmed out to contractors who paid the royal government lump sums and collected the taxes in question, often profiting extensively in the process. The system was complex, inefficient and abusive. The term *ferme* is applied either to the entire system or a portion of it. The contractors were called *fermiers*, the highest ranking being *fermiers généraux*.

Lettre de cachet. A letter or order signed by the king, countersigned by a minister and sealed with the royal seal. A favorite means of direct exercise of the royal authority.

Lit de justice. Ceremony during which the king came into the Parlement, reassumed the powers that he had delegated to it, and ordered the registration of one or more edicts or ordinances which the Parlement had refused to accept.

Livre (monetary unit) Silver coin valued at 20 *sous*.

Parlements. The highest or "sovereign" courts in the French system of permanent tribunals. They could be overridden only by the king or his council. In addition to their judicial functions, the Parlements "verified" all new royal edicts and ordinances by enregistering them, thereby permitting them to become law. It was a rudimentary type of judicial review and acted as a check on royal legislation. If a Parlement disapproved of an enactment for legal or other reasons, it might send remonstrances to the king whereupon lengthy negotiations ensued. If the king wished to force the issue, he might come into the Parlement and hold a *lit de justice*, ordering registration of the new laws. The Parlement of Paris was by far the most important such body and exercised jurisdiction over about one-half of the realm; various provinces also had Parlements with corresponding powers. Louis XIV in effect abolished the Parlements' political powers and limited them to trying cases between subjects.

Paulette. The *paulette* or *droit annuel* was established in 1604 and was an annual payment by holders of venal offices, one-sixtieth of their value. Heretofore many offices had been venal but not fully inheritable as other properties; the payment ensured that the officeholder might transmit his office to his heirs. The *paulette* tended to strengthen the practice of venality and was often criticized for this reason. It received its name from its originator, Charles Paulet, a minor administrator.

Pistole. Spanish gold coin. Valued at approximately 10 *livres*.

Présidiaux. Royal courts established in the sixteenth century in most of the *bailliages* and *sénéchaussées.*

Prévôt. Name given to a large variety of royal agents who exercised various administrative, military and/or judicial powers in local areas.

Sénéchaussée. Territory in southern France administered by a *sénéchal,* a royal official. Similar to the *bailliage* in northern France.

Taille. The most important direct royal tax. Theoretically paid by all but the privileged classes, but was especially burdensome on the peasants and the workers in the cities. Assessment was based on a given person's holding (*taille personnelle*) or directly upon properties (*taille réelle*), the latter being the more efficient.